RED DIRT AND GOLD DUST

LINDY PRICE

RED DIRT AND GOLD DUST

Copyright © 2025 by Lindy Price

All rights reserved. No part of this book may be reproduced in any manner whatsoever without written permission except in the case of brief quotations embodied in critical articles and reviews.

First Printing by Ingram Spark, 2025
First published by Bekker Media, 2025

ISBN: 978-1-7641247-4-4
eISBN: 978-1-7641247-3-7

Unless otherwise stated, all scriptures are taken from the NEW INTERNATIONAL VERSION (NIV): Scripture taken from THE HOLY BIBLE, NEW INTERNATIONAL VERSION ®. Copyright© 1973, 1978, 1984, 2011 by Biblica, Inc.™. Used by permission of Zondervan

Scriptures marked NKJV are taken from the NEW KING JAMES VERSION (NKJV): Scripture taken from the NEW KING JAMES VERSION®. Copyright© 1982 by Thomas Nelson, Inc. Used by permission. All rights reserved.

Scripture quotations taken from the Amplified® Bible (AMPC), Copyright © 1954, 1958, 1962, 1964, 1965, 1987 by The Lockman Foundation Used by permission. www.lockman.org.

Cover design by Bekker Media. Cover image generated using ChatGPT from the prompt "girl and a horse with dog by her side, outback sunset."
Edited by Bekker Media, New South Wales.

A copy of this title is held at the National Library of Australia.

GEOGRAPHIC LOCATIONS OF MY VETERINARY CAREER

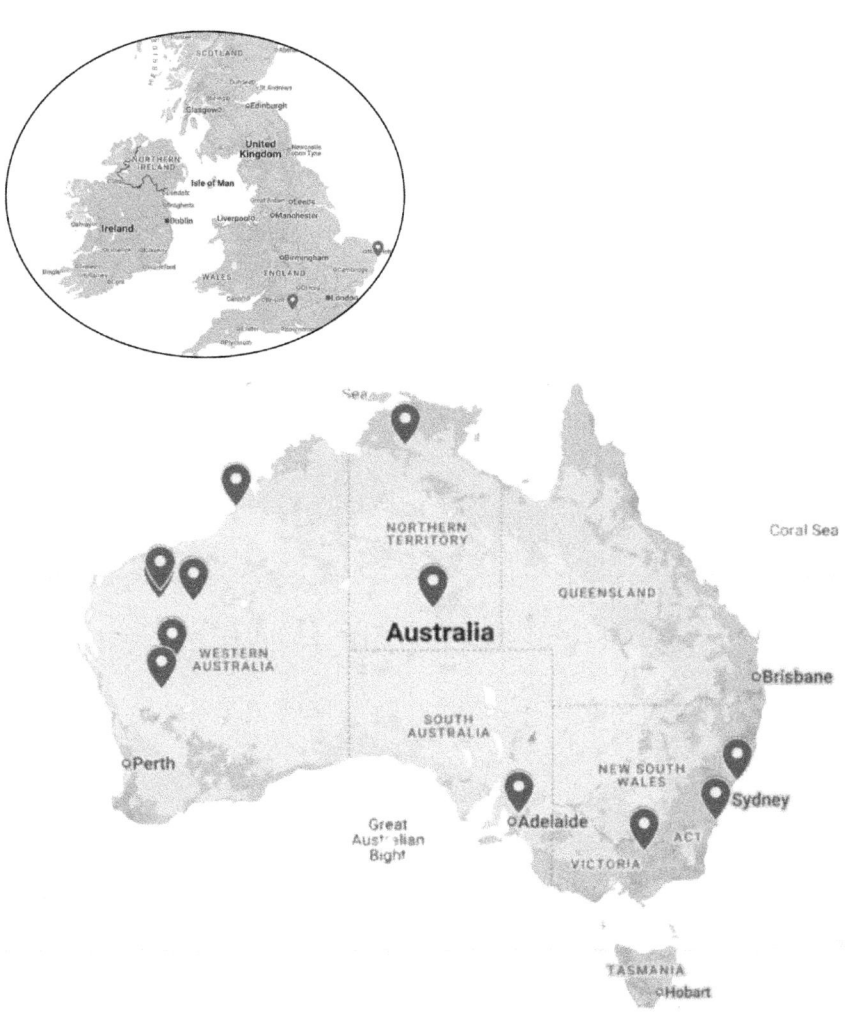

CONTENTS

Dedication
x
Acknowledgements
xi

— Introduction
1

— Part One - A WOUNDED SOUL
5

1 — An Abscess Of The Soul
7

2 — Love Deficiency
11

3 — The Insanity Of Running
17

4 — Toughen Up
21

5 — Stepping Out Of The Cage
27

6 — When Your Best Is Not Good Enough
37

7 — Toxic As A Snake Bite
43

— Part Two - UNDIAGNOSED SOUL WOUNDS
49

8 — Numbing The Pain
51

9 — Distraction
53

10 — Performance In Career
57

11 — Travel And Adventure
61

12 — Danger (Risk Taking)
65

13 — Dysfunction (Walking With A Limp)
75

14 — Disablement (Avoidance And Amputation)
79

15 — The Damage Of A Misdiagnosis
81

16 — Love Substitution
83

— Part Three - HEALING OF A WOUNDED SOUL
87

17 — Rain In The Desert
89

18 — Baking A Cake Without A Recipe
97

19 — Building On A Rock
105

20 – Gold Dust
115

21 – Heart Restoration
123

22 – A Firm Place To Stand
129

23 – Dealing With Addiction
135

24 – In The Round Yard With Jesus
141

25 – Great Signposts But Terrible Masters
149

26 – God's Way Is Better Than My Way
155

27 – Light Accelerates Healing
161

28 – For Veterinarians
169

Appendix
174

Red Dirt and Gold Dust is dedicated to my husband Mal,
my son Liam and my daughter Olivia.
Your love and support bring joy to my life.

ACKNOWLEDGEMENTS

I would like to thank all of my veterinary employers over the years. You have all helped me to grow and learn and I applaud your contributions to the veterinary industry. To Rick, Debbie, Sam, Malcolm, Alan, Cathy, Dave, Fiona, Chris, Lionel, David, Felicity, Karen, Chris and Martin, may you be blessed in all that you do.

To all of my dear veterinary colleagues and veterinary nurse friends, I truly appreciate you. Working with you and working through the good days and bad days is always better when we do it together.

For all of my colleagues and friends on a journey to find peace, may you seek and find everything you are looking for and more.

INTRODUCTION

Red Dirt and Gold Dust weaves together multiple stories, and I would like to provide some context for the way they have been told.

Ever since I was in primary school, I have wanted to be a veterinary surgeon. I first declared that I wanted to become a vet in Grade 6 as a twelve-year-old and my career aspirations never really wavered from that point on. For the greater part of my life, I have been immersed in the diagnosis, treatment, care and rehabilitation of animals, especially family pets.

I have also been a concrete thinker for the greater part of my life, and a highly visual and experiential learner. It makes perfect sense to me to tell my story using animals, their illnesses and injuries and true stories from my life as a vet working across Australia, to explain concepts that may otherwise be abstract.

A prime motivation for telling my story is to shed light on various important issues, some of which are common to the general population, and some that are unique to the veterinary profession. It is my hope to raise awareness of the impacts of trauma, childhood sexual abuse and domestic violence and to provide hope for recovery for people who have experienced them.

While it is simple to understand an injury to the body such as a broken bone or a laceration requiring stitches, it is much harder to understand an injury to the soul. Throughout this story I would like you to think of the soul as the mind, will or attitude and emotions. Trauma, sexual abuse, sexual violence and domestic violence injure the soul.

To understand a soul injury you need to consider how these experiences can impact the thought processes, self-esteem, confidence and behaviour of an individual. The best way I know how to describe my life experiences with trauma is to give you an analogy from the veterinary world that is easier to relate to. I want to stress that this is my personal experience, and I don't intend in any way to diminish other people's experiences of trauma. But I do hope that using analogies will allow you to understand the ways that these traumas have impacted my life.

Names of my clients and their animals have been changed to protect their privacy, but the stories represent actual events that have occurred throughout my veterinary career.

I also want to note at this point that I have been a veterinarian for thirty years. The industry has grown, developed and changed dramatically over that time. My stories do not represent current thinking or standards of best practice. Instead, they represent the gritty truth of working in an intensely challenging occupation in extremely challenging locations across rural and remote Australia.

Because the veterinary industry in Australia is so small, it is much harder for me to protect the identity of my employers because there are often only one or two vets in small country towns. I want to take this opportunity to honour and thank my past employers who have all contributed to my career, helping me to grow and learn and become the vet I am today.

The book has three main sections:

-The first section of the book tells the stories of the wounding process.

-The second part of the book tells the story of my very best attempts to live my life without dealing with the wounds.

-The last part of the book tells the story of my healing and restoration - my rehabilitation.

I don't want to re-traumatise people who have experienced trauma themselves, so I intentionally don't cover any detail from the episodes of sexual trauma or domestic violence. But I do want my readers to understand the mental processing that accompanies those injuries and the way that I found freedom from them, to provide hope for others on a healing journey.

So - spoiler alert, the story is rough, but it gets better ... and there is peace and freedom at the end.

PART ONE - A WOUNDED SOUL

CHAPTER 1

AN ABSCESS OF THE SOUL

CHILDHOOD TRAUMA IS LIKE A DOG FIGHT WOUND IN THE TERRITORY

Dog fights are nasty. The canine teeth frequently pierce the skin, injecting bacteria from the mouth deep into the wounds. Once dogs have a grip on their opponent, they shake their victim from side to side. The tissues are torn, bruised and crushed. The wound itself may look innocuous - just a small collection of puncture wounds, but the damage is all lurking below the surface and, left untreated, can be life threatening.

In the tropics, dog fight wounds are more serious because the infection blooms into an abscess in a very short space of time. The temperature in the tropical north of Australia is hot. In the dry season it is hot and dry. In the wet season it is hot and humid, and when it rains, it becomes hot and wet. After the rain, the mud steams and it becomes hot and humid again. The cocktail of bacteria in the tropics is potent and deadly and it loves the heat.

Massive tissue damage is a perfect environment for bacterial growth, and sepsis (or blood poisoning) is a real concern. On top of that, the lag time between injury and the medical attention required may more often be days rather than hours, because of the distance between the incident with the dog and available veterinary care. In the outback, many people live hours away from the clinic; miles away down long dirt roads that would take a day to navigate for a veterinary visit. For this reason, many owners try to resolve the injury themselves with some disinfectant and a good hose down, before committing to a day of travel to get help for their dogs. Delaying treatment with antibiotics in the tropics is never wise.

Just like a dog fight wound in the Territory, childhood sexual abuse creates a wound in the soul that if left untreated creates a life-threatening contamination of thoughts, emotions and attitude. The time scale, however, is vastly different. Soul injuries sustained in childhood can suppurate for years. The time between injury and treatment can be decades.

Childhood trauma is especially difficult to manage, because there may be no external injuries. You can't treat what you can't see. No-one could see the damage to my soul when I was a kid. But the insidious thoughts gained an entry point, just like damaging bacteria injected deep into a wound. Those thought patterns festered into an abscess in my soul.

'There's something wrong with me'
'I feel dirty.'
'Don't tell.'
'If people find out they won't like you.'
'I don't fit in.'
'I am not good enough.'

While other kids were developing trust in their family connections, feeling safe and secure, I felt like there was something wrong with me. I didn't fit in. The insidious thought patterns became beliefs, established and reinforced by my experiences in life. I grew up with a very low opinion of myself, craving affirmation. I felt like I could only please my Mum if I succeeded in school. So, I participated in school and life as best as I could, trying to please my parents at every turn. I played sport, learnt music and did well at my studies. When I was successful, I felt loved. I ached for love, which supercharged my drive to be successful in my studies.

The affirmation certainly started coming with the A grades on the report card, so I established a way to earn approval and kept working hard for it. I was about twelve years old when I decided I would like to become a vet. Everyone told me that it was a difficult course to get into, and I would have to work hard. So, I did. From that point on I developed a singular focus to attain entry into veterinary school.

Halfway through my final year at school I developed glandular fever, and all bets were off. I was stuck at home for weeks, communicating with only a handful of my teachers and trying to finish off the classwork from my bed. It looked as if there was no hope of me attaining my dreams. However, as fate would have it, there was to be no intake for the veterinary science degree the following year, since Melbourne University was trialling a new system. Prospective students would be selected from first year science. I enrolled in a science degree at Melbourne Uni and one year later, I was accepted into Veterinary School. My Dad wept with pride. My Mum said, 'I do hope you'll be trying for honours'.

I was filled with joy and anger at the same time. Would I ever be good enough for her?

CHAPTER 2

LOVE DEFICIENCY

...A CRITICAL CONDITION OF THE SOUL.

One day, while I was working in Katherine, I was excited to get a callout to visit a cow. It was very unusual to be called to a single animal in the Northern Territory, because of the cost of travel and the vast distances between patients. I thought that this must be a fairly valuable cow!

I had two work experience students with me, so we bundled into my single cab Hilux and headed south. It was about a 100 km each way

The cow was ready and waiting for me in the yards when I arrived. I put on my overalls, grabbed my medical kit from the car, and made my way over to the crush (the cattle race where the cow was confined), with the students in tow.

The cow was standing in the crush already, head hanging low and mouth open. She looked pretty unwell. I told the station owner that I needed to feel in her mouth to see what was going on. I rolled up my sleeves, sidled up to the cow like my university lecturer had taught me, and cradled the cow's head with one hand while sliding my other hand into her mouth. Two things bothered me immediately. Firstly, I could feel a bone jammed in the back of the cow's throat. And secondly, I felt an unpleasant crawling sensation on my hand. I withdrew my hand from the cow's mouth and to my utter horror and disgust, brought a handful of maggots with me.

The station owner retreated to the far end of the yard and was bent over gagging.

I was reeling from the sight of my arm coated in maggots and was feverishly brushing them off my arm and my overalls. I proceeded to slap myself all over because I was paranoid that I was covered in maggots.

It took me some time to regain my composure. My skin was crawling, and my natural inclination was to join the station owner in evacuating my stomach contents. I drew breath, swigged on my water bottle and surveyed the situation. My next challenge was how to remove the bone - it was so firmly wedged in the cow's mouth.

Armed with two ropes, I had one student stand on the top of the crush and apply pressure to a rope passing through the cow's mouth, securing the upper jaw. I had a second rope and the other student applying pressure to the lower jaw, so that I could start to manipulate the cow's mouth more effectively. I donned long gloves. I double-gloved and put on a spare apron I occasionally used for preg-testing cows.

Grimacing, and trying desperately to ignore the maggots dripping from the cow's mouth, I again stuck my hand into the cow's mouth and started to dislodge the bone. The bone was firmly wedged to the upper palate. As it started to come away, I was a little anxious that some of the cow's hard palate was coming away with it. With some added muscle from the students and enough space for manoeuvring, the bone finally came free.

The station owner who had been missing in action, returned with a bottle of Listerine in his pocket. I wasn't sure if it was for him or the cow. We hosed the remaining maggots off the cow, gave her a shot of antibiotics and instructions for the station owner to give a full course, and released her from the crush to go and drink her fill.

'Pica' is the term we use for a depraved appetite. It is the result of a nutritionally deficient diet. The lack of certain minerals - in this case, phosphorus - leads to a desperation that lacks discernment. This particular cow had attempted to restore phosphorus levels by eating the bones of a carcass. The problem is that cows are not designed to eat bones, and one of them had lodged in her mouth, leaving her unable to eat or drink. This unfortunate cow's desperation for nutrients could have killed her.

***

My childhood had left me with a less obvious deficiency - a deficiency of the soul. I had a love deficit. Every child needs to be loved. My need hadn't been fully satisfied, and the abuse I had experienced compounded my lack. Just like a cow with pica, I was desperate for love and acceptance, and I had no discernment. I sought ways to satisfy this deficiency in a range of ways that were dangerous and destructive.

My first job was in Western Australia. With my degree in hand, I was up for adventure and ready to strike out on my own. I literally drove as far across the country as I could, to put some miles between me and my family of origin, and the past that I didn't want to acknowledge. I landed in a mining town in the Pilbara region of Western Australia. The population was mostly male, who were also starved of love. It was a toxic mix of elements, all marinating in drugs and alcohol. It was there that I started my life as an outback vet.

My job was full of challenges unique to our remote location. The clinic I was working in was a base for the region. Each week, either I or my colleague would drive long distances to run outback clinics for clients in these remote mining towns.

One week I would drive 600 km south and treat animals in three different towns. The next week, I would go north and east and drive four to five hours on dirt roads to treat animals in two more towns. It was exhausting work, so we would take it in turns to do the trips while the other vet stayed home to man the clinic. We were either on the road or on call, all the time.

The conditions were hot. One day, on a routine visit to Paraburdoo where I worked in a little caravan beside the hospital, I accidentally left my thermometer on. It read the temperature inside the van and came up with an error message, because the temperature was over 43 degrees Celsius.

It was hot, thirsty work and I frequently found myself having a few cold beers with the locals after work. As a result, I found myself in positions of risk and vulnerability. While I, on the one hand, had a love deficit and a heart aching for intimacy, the men in those mining towns just wanted a quick one-night stand. Commitment was a dirty word in those hot, dry and dusty places.

Dating was also fraught with difficulty. The town was so small that most people knew everyone's business and there were a limited number of places to go for a private date and to get to know someone. Consequently, it became a much better option to go for a drive and check out a remote waterhole or swimming spot. This strategy, however, was to have disastrous consequences for me. One toxic relationship led to a string of bad encounters, culminating in date rape in a remote community.

I was not equipped to deal with that kind of pain. No-one is. I tried to ignore my wounds and focus my mind on my job. Occasionally the pain in my soul would break through in outbursts of anger, but mostly it was directed inwardly, expressed in a damaging internal narrative stuck on repeat.

Trying to ignore my problem and my pain only seemed to escalate it. I had not committed to a relationship with this man, but I was like a dingo with my foot stuck in a dog trap. The more I struggled to free myself from his romantic interest, the more it hurt.

He didn't take no for an answer, and he began to stalk me in that tiny town. I would wake at three in the morning with headlights on high beam flooding my room. Whenever I walked my dog, his ute would appear. Whenever I tried to go for a drive out of town, I would be tailed. There was no escape. He bought a dog so that he could see me for his dog's veterinary care. I wasn't even sure if I could refuse to see him. I decided to do as many of the remote visits as I could, because staying in town became untenable. I worked long hours in tough conditions and a few short months later, I had exhausted all of my physical, emotional and mental reserves.

I resigned from my first position in the outback. I didn't tell my boss or the police about my stalker. My boss was disappointed. He told me that I was 'a disgrace to myself and my family'. In that moment I believed him. Those words sunk deep into my soul and lingered, hidden in my heart for many years.

THE INSANITY OF RUNNING

The definition of insanity is repeating the same thing and expecting a different result. The next man seemed charming, capable and caring. I still needed to be loved; my soul was crying out for love. I also needed to get away from the pain of my romantic failure. Despite my raw romantic wounds and my reluctance to trust again, my life seemed to be inexorably drawn towards this man. He was chivalrous, charismatic and well liked in the bush town where I met him. He knew how to fix things. He worked in the field with mining exploration teams. And I was still desperate for love and for protection. And I needed a change.

We embarked on an adventure to a new job in a new state and we drove through some of the wildest and most beautiful terrain in Australia to get there. We camped in desert gorges, explored the Kimberley wilderness, hiked through the Bungle Bungles and drove long dusty days to a new job in Alice Springs, right in the heart of Australia.

The red flags were there at the beginning. We fought over music. We fought over campsites, dinners and minor decisions. Fights would be ugly. Sometimes sharp objects were thrown. Sometimes expensive photographic equipment was smashed. It was only bearable when we would drink too much, tearily apologise over a bottle of red wine ... or two, and vow never to repeat the routine. I told myself I was stressed about my new job and that this too would pass.

Entering into a violent relationship is less of a choice and more of an entrapment. You need a functioning identity, a sense of self-worth and self-esteem to be able to discern character in a new relationship. I had no means of escaping my situation because I was paralysed by indecision and fear. Even though I had an inner voice telling me that it was a bad choice, I had no sounding board; no-one around me who could speak with wisdom into my situation. When those faculties of identity and self-esteem are eroded by trauma, violence or abuse it can leave you blind to the truth. I was utterly unable to help myself at that moment. It was like walking into the lion's den and expecting that everything would be okay. I stayed in that relationship because I felt vulnerable and incapable on my own. I didn't have the courage or resources to manage conflict, address wounds or have a meaningful conversation about mutual respect. I passively entered into the most damaging eighteen months of my life.

Amid the turmoil of domestic violence, I threw myself into my work. I was determined to succeed in some area of my life. My boss in Alice Springs was a highly respected veterinarian and she had plenty to teach me as I continued to find my feet as a new graduate. She made herself available to me when I was on call, she supported me as I learned new techniques, and I worked in a team that were focused on quality medicine and surgery and excellence in patient care. Even in this environment, I couldn't flourish. I found it hard to work in a team. I took feedback as personal criticism. I was miserable and I believed that I wasn't cut out to be a vet.

Coupled with that, I made some fairly horrendous medical blunders. Because I didn't have the confidence to have collaborative case discussions, I would make bad decisions in isolation, despite having people around me who could have advised me. My boss would come along behind me and mop up the mess. I felt undermined and inadequate but couldn't learn from my blunders either. I had a deeply entrenched fear of failure, and every time I made a mistake, I felt a failure. I was so fiercely independent that asking for help didn't occur to me. I didn't want to ask for help because I figured that it was a sign of weakness. I had a degree, so I should be able to do this, right?

In my first job, I had made my own decisions, with my boss 1200 km away on the phone. In this job I was making my own decisions but was being constantly scrutinised and corrected by a boss listening from the next room. The narrative in my head just got worse. I was struggling at work and struggling at home. I had moments of peace when my man worked away, and weeks of intense misery and alcohol abuse when he was back. Whichever way I turned, I felt like I was failing.

I was unable to take responsibility for my challenges, so I blamed my boss for the disillusionment I was feeling. That way the problem was neither myself nor my toxic relationship - it was my workplace. So once again, I left my job, seeking peace in another workplace, another location, another tiny town in the outback.

What I didn't know at the time (it would take me years to learn), was that you don't find peace in places or people. My joy was my responsibility. No human can fill the hole in your heart to make you whole. Domestic violence left my soul dark and desperate and my eyes dull. There were gaping holes where my dreams and hopes and aspirations used to shine. There was just darkness against a toxic background of violent interaction. Survival was my only goal. Joy was a distant memory and cortisol spikes were my daily reality.

TOUGHEN UP

If Australia has a wild west, it has to be Katherine in the Northern Territory. It sure was a wild ride while I lived there. My boss was as tough as they come, both inside and out. She interviewed me one Friday afternoon and introduced me to the hitherto unknown pleasure of XXXX beer. A whole case later, we agreed on the terms and conditions of my employment and set a start date. But while I was running away from Alice Springs, I ran away from none of my problems. I carefully packed up all of my disasters and mental hang-ups, including my deeply troubled and abusive relationship, and brought them with me in my Hilux to Katherine.

The job in Katherine was an exciting mix of clinic-based work, cattle work and remote Indigenous community visits. I was keen to try my hand at a larger variety of cases, including cattle work. Maybe, I thought to myself, including large animals in my working caseload would increase my work satisfaction and fulfilment.

My first day on the job was brutal. I arrived in Katherine in January, after a 5700 km road trip back home to Wangaratta via Alice Springs, and then back up north from Wangaratta to Katherine. I was staying with my boss for the first few weeks until I could find some accommodation. The first night in Katherine we ate dinner and talked late into the evening, enjoying beers and then later some red wine to lubricate the conversation.

I woke to my alarm after a fitful night's sleep on a waterbed that had threatened to buck me off all night. I had a hangover, and I was also nervous. I had no idea what export cattle work in the Territory would be like.

The sun was still some way off rising as we drove down my boss's driveway to our job at an export cattle yard. It was the wet season. As the sun rose, the temperature soared to thirty-eight degrees Celsius, the humidity hovered around 98 % and the steam rose off the mud along the cattle race as I started to question the wisdom of my latest job application. My head throbbed and I felt like I might vomit. We had two thousand head of cattle to inspect, vaccinate and treat for ticks before the day was out.

My boss seemed invincible. She was not affected by the temperature or the alcohol consumption the night before. She introduced me to the exporters and the station hands and got to work straight away. And so, it began. The station hands would load up a race of steers and lock them in place. My boss and I vaccinated the cattle in their flanks, and they jostled and jumped and snorted with indignation as we needled them. They were barely domesticated Brahman cattle, as tall as I was and six times my weight. Then we would deliver the tick treatment via spring-loaded back line guns, delivering around 40 ml of medication with each squeeze. There was a lag time as the spring-loaded mechanism refilled the barrel of the gun, so we used two, one for each hand. The race gate was opened and as the cattle ran past, we sprayed them with the tick treatment.

Then we repeated the process, literally running up and down the cattle race, vaccinating and treating cattle for what seemed like an eternity. The mud stuck to the soles of my boots and got heavier and heavier as my legs started to cramp. There was no time for toilet breaks, and also no need, as I became as dry as a chip. My hands began to ache with the effort required to squeeze the vaccinating guns and my arms started to feel slightly numb with the effort.

I was hopelessly unprepared for the physical effort of the work in Katherine and completely perplexed that anyone could do that kind of work, day in, day out and not die. At the end of that first day, my boss smiled at me with a wry grin and told me that I might need to 'toughen up'. Then we went home, and she offered me a beer….it was thirsty work.

It took me a good three days to recover from my first day at work. My muscles seized and I was lactic beyond repair. I could barely walk, at least not without an awkward grimace and some prehistoric groans. I generously offered to man the clinic for the rest of the week, sucking up the air conditioning like a true southerner, and learning the routines of the small animal side of the business.

My second day was not much better. My boss showed me around the consulting room, surgery and treatment areas in the clinic and the hospital cages out the back. My first case was a sweet mother cat, nursing four kittens. My boss told me that she was a stray and asked me to euthanise her and the kittens, and then she left me to it.

I understand that feral cats and stray cats are insatiable hunters. I understand that councils don't have the means or the desire to control stray cat populations. I understand that people are irresponsible and let their cats have multiple litters. I also understand that feral and stray cats have decimated wildlife populations and are responsible for extinctions of species in great swathes of land in the north of Australia. But in that moment, I couldn't do it. And I am not even a cat person. I am a dog person. Cats barely tolerate me at the best of times. They seem to know that I am a dog person. This cat was different though. She was on a survival mission. She smooched into my shoulder and started to purr. My heart melted in that moment, and my mind raced for a plausible alternative. I was not going to impress my boss on day two either.

I sheepishly approached the office where she was doing some paperwork. I asked her if we could re-home the mother cat and her kittens. My boss sighed, rolled her eyes and told me...'you are going to have to toughen up'. And that was that. We found a home for one kitten. The practice manager's parents took the mother cat, another nurse took one kitten, and I kept the remaining two kittens. Those two cats provided me with love and joy like their life depended on it. They were 'dog-like' cats. They would follow me in the garden. They would walk with me to the corner store. And when it was time to sit in front of the TV at night, they would lie on my chest and purr and drool until it was time for bed.

I settled into a sort of rhythm in Katherine. I worked hard. I shared the on-call duties with my boss, so I was on call approximately half the time. The cattle work was seasonal, but when it was busy, it was exhausting. The small animal business provided me with ample challenges to strengthen my surgical and medical skills, and I had the opportunity to do remote clinics in communities around Katherine in the dry season.

My personal life settled into an uneasy pattern as well. My partner would work away for three weeks at a time and return to Katherine for a week off. When he was back, we would drink too much, and invariably we would fight. When he was away, he became angry if I wasn't home to take his call. When he was home, we would have endless arguments about things I can't even remember. There were late nights, smashed plates and early morning apologies.

All this against the backdrop of the consistent busyness of my work, I quickly became emotionally and physically exhausted. The problem with running away (especially from yourself) is that everywhere you go ... there you are.

CHAPTER 5

STEPPING OUT OF THE CAGE

While I have a deep affection for many animals, marine turtles potentially being at the top of that list, nothing breaks my heart like a traumatised puppy. It sits in the back of the cage, trying not to make eye contact. The bedding is all scrunched up and it sits as far away from the humans as it can get. The whites of its eyes flash as the puppy takes a glance towards the door, then stares at the wall, every fibre of its being hoping that no-one will notice them or come and open the door.

When the door is opened the terror inside the puppy reaches a crescendo. The whites of its eyes are not enough to deter the vet or the vet nurse. The lip is lifted in a snarl and a low growl starts to rumble from deep in its belly: *Please stay away from me.* It dodges the lead and snaps at the approaching hands. The hands that are trying to help look just like the hands that have hurt them in the past. Because there is nowhere to flee, the puppy fights, snapping at flesh like a land shark.

The cage door opens and the humans step back. A piece of chicken is on the floor. Even with a juicy treat and no immediate threat, it takes enormous courage for that little dog to step out of the cage.

To say that my first few years in veterinary practice were tumultuous is an understatement: they were traumatic. Apart from starting a very challenging career, I had experienced sexual violence, a stalker and domestic violence. I had moved three times over vast distances in the space of two years and had lived and worked in remote outback towns and locations.

I was also able to step out of the cage of a deeply abusive relationship in Katherine. I am honestly not able to tell how I did it. I continued to live and work in that town, clutching onto any familiarity and friendships in my workplace as I counted the cost, both emotionally and financially, of the previous eighteen months.

I was just starting to find a rhythm in my veterinary life when everyone's life in Katherine was about to change. It was January 26th, Australia Day, 1998. Australia was playing South Africa in a one-day cricket game and, with the weather coming in, most people had settled in front of the TV with a cleansing ale. I, however, was on call. It had been raining solidly for two days, and the locals were keeping a close eye on the river levels in Katherine Gorge. An ex-tropical cyclone had settled over Arnhem Land and was dumping rain on the Katherine river catchment. While the gossip around town speculated about flooding, I was wondering how damaging an ex-tropical cyclone could possibly be.

My first emergency call of the day came through around mid-morning. A little dog had broken its leg while being hauled out of flood waters into a little tinny (small fishing boat), near the low-lying caravan park. His owner was extremely stressed. He was having to evacuate his house and was anxious for me to fix his dog, right then and there, so that he wouldn't have to leave him in the hospital. I x-rayed the leg and found that the radius and ulna were broken. Normally I would bandage the limb for support and consider surgical options for repair in the days ahead. We would need to prepare equipment and possibly order in supplies to carry out the procedure. But not this time. At the owner's urgings, I placed a cast on the leg and recovered his dog from anaesthetic. He paid his bill and left with his fairly groggy dog, to pack up his house 'before it was all too late'.

I was perplexed. Yes, it was raining, but was I missing something? Did he know something I didn't? I tidied up the clinic and was just locking up when a policeman approached, knocking on the front door. He was wide-eyed and anxious.

'You have to evacuate', he told me with an unnerving degree of urgency. 'The river has gone eight metres in the gorge - the town is going to flood'.

I had no idea what to expect, so I rang my boss. She lived out of town on a property. She was already flooded in, but it took a lot to alarm my boss. She told me to relax; everything would be okay. I was wondering if I should move lower-lying items onto the benchtops, or up higher. My boss wasn't too concerned but also had no capacity to help me - so she encouraged me to go back home and hunker down until the storm passed.

I did a quick sweep through the clinic. I grabbed a few pieces of critical equipment, including intravenous fluids and catheters, tape and bandaging supplies and I packed the 'horse box' (a large plastic box with basic first aid, bandages, medications and medical supplies). Just as I was about to walk out the door, I heard a plaintiff meow from the cattery. Arthur, a handsome tabby cat, was in the clinic boarding, while his owners were away. While I was standing in front of his cage, I had a visual image of flood waters inundating the clinic and Arthur being trapped in his low-level cage, unable to escape. It sent a chill down my spine. I scooped Arthur up out of the bottom cage and placed him at head height instead. I also filled his bowls full of food and water in case the predictions were right, and I wasn't able to get back for a while. It didn't occur to me that the water level could reach head height in the clinic, so for now I considered him safe.

As I left the clinic, and drove through town to my home in Katherine East, there were mixed reactions to the evacuation order. Some people were feverishly moving things, including cars and valuables to high ground, or packing sandbags and trying to protect homes or businesses. Others were sitting on their verandas, watching the cricket. It didn't 'feel' like there was an impending disaster.

It rained solidly all day and all night, as it can in the tropics. I woke the next day, ready to go back to work. As I drove out of my street, it took me only moments to realise that today would be a day like no other. There was water as far as the eye could see. The roads leading from Katherine East into town were closed. There were roadblocks, police and the SES in numbers were standing at the water's edge. I looked further into the floodwaters to see a stream of little tinnies ferrying people and goods from town, back to high ground. A policeman approached my car and told me to turn around; there wasn't any work for anyone today except to rescue people off the roofs of their houses.

I had never been in a natural disaster like this before. Yes, it had flooded in my hometown of Wangaratta when I was growing up, but on a scale so vastly different to this that it was incomparable. I had no idea what to do. On one hand I was quite pleased to have the day off work. But when I was sitting at home, all I wanted was to be busy. It didn't seem right to be sitting still.

Our little share house had tripled its occupants the day before. My friend who worked at the DPI (Department of Primary Industries) offered our lounge room to a couple who had been evacuated early in the day, and I shared my room with a friend from the CBD area of town. We sat around listening to the local radio station, trying to figure out what was next. In between games of Monopoly and UNO, we anxiously contemplated where our next meal was coming from - we had neglected to do any shopping the day before, so the fridge was bare.

By mid-afternoon, I had a horrible thought. What about Arthur, the cat I had left in the clinic the day before? My heart rate doubled, and I had a knot of anxiety curling into a tight ball in my stomach. I should go and get him. While it was still pouring with rain, I drove back down to the water's edge and spoke to one of the emergency personnel. There were army officers, helicopters buzzing overhead and a whole lot more boats in the water, still ferrying people. I explained that I was a vet and needed to get into the clinic to rescue a patient and to get more supplies. We had started accumulating lost dogs in our backyard and it occurred to me that we should also get some food while we could. I had also spoken to my boss, isolated by flood waters out of town. She was trying to help horses and livestock that had received cuts while swimming through floodwaters, trying to get to higher ground. I needed to grab some tetanus shots, antibiotics, and suture kits from the clinic so that I could get them to her.

I waited for a while, as the police and the emergency team discussed some options. Before long, I was in the queue to take a ride in a boat back into the flood zone to get some urgent veterinary supplies.

I grew up waterskiing and boating all of my life, but that particular boat ride was the most shocking experience I have ever had on the water. As we motored away from the water's edge, the current began to exert pressure on the boat. In order to keep the boat going in the right direction, heading north into town, the SES driver had to push the nose into the current. We were virtually full throttle, facing into the current, going sideways along the main road into town, in nearly two metres of water.

I could barely take in the scene around me. There were gas bottles floating along in the current, hissing and spewing their contents into the water. The water was thick with debris, tree trunks, branches, fridges, washing machines and cars making their way downstream. At one point a terrified, wide-eyed cow swam past us, panicked and exhausted. I looked urgently at the driver of our boat, and he just made a tight line with his lips and shook his head.

'No way.'

As we approached the main intersection of town, our driver told me to 'hang on'. I was wondering why I would have to hang on, then realised that we would have to go upstream. We took a right turn at the traffic lights. The lights were flashing red, the green light was still visible above the water… just. The businesses lining the main street were submerged to the level of the street awnings or roofs. We rounded the corner, and the SES driver gunned the engine. We were now heading up Gorge Road, full throttle into the current.

Fortunately, the water level began to drop as we approached the clinic, which was slightly protected from the full force of the floodwaters. We edged our way into the clinic carpark, and I got out. The water was hip deep. I grabbed the clinic keys and opened the door, struggling against a wad of material on the other side of the door. The clinic had been inundated to the level of the bench tops. The new computers had a film of brown sludge. One stand of dog food had toppled over, and a couple of bags of food had burst open. The dog food had swollen to create large, floating, festering baubles of food, floating in the foetid mess in the clinic. There were consumable items like needles and syringes, floating in the water, that had made their way from the storeroom into the waiting area. The whole building was wet. Humidity meant that the interior was dripping, even if it wasn't covered with floodwater. The smell was a rich cocktail of fermenting food and sewer mud. And in the back of the clinic came that same, plaintiff meow. Arthur was okay.

I grabbed a carry cage, and Arthur was extremely compliant as I bundled him into the cage and put him on the top of the counter. The fridge that I had hoped to grab some tetanus shots from was partially toppled over and its contents were bobbing in the water in the consulting room. The tetanus vaccinations were warm ... and non-viable. I salvaged some cat food for Arthur and as many bags of dog food as the tinny would carry. Any medications and injectables that were not floating in the soup in the clinic, I threw into a plastic bag and loaded onto the boat. The SES and emergency volunteers helped me grab as much as I could before I left. They were doubtful that I would get an opportunity to get back to the clinic until the flood waters receded ... and at that point, no-one knew when that would be.

The trip back out of town was just as horrifying as the trip into town. On the way back we stopped in at the supermarket. Waist deep in water, at a side entry of the main supermarket in town, were a couple of men loading tins and non-perishable items into boats. An alarm was sounding somewhere back in the store and the water was over a metre deep throughout. The supermarket was completely flooded. There were teams of people ferrying canned and bottled items and food that wasn't spoilt. The evacuation centre needed food. Baked beans, spaghetti, gherkins - whatever wasn't broken was salvaged where possible. Loaded to the brim and with Arthur complaining loudly on my lap in the cage, we made our way back to dry land ... back through the current, running the gauntlet between submerged cars, terrified livestock and debris that would have been in someone's backyard the day before.

The next step was to get supplies to my boss. My vet nurse was always good value, so I rang her, reporting on the state of the clinic and to see if she had any ideas. Kate was a Territorian, born and bred. She was one of a big family and she never seemed to get flustered. Whenever I greeted her at work in the morning, and asked how she was, she would shoot me a wry smile and say... 'goin' steady'.

She asked if I was afraid of heights, and I said no. Then she suggested I take a ride with her brother. I met her near the police station in a paddock, with a plastic box full of medical supplies for horses, cattle and the dogs and cats that had been rescued from the floodwater out of town.

Then Kate's brother showed up. He was a pilot for Helimuster, and he was running supplies to the isolated people and homesteads out of town. He was flying a 'Robbo'. These are the mustering helicopters that look like a plastic bubble with a lawn mower engine and a flywheel for a propeller. They don't have doors, and they are tiny. There's really only room for one and a bit people. I was suddenly afraid of heights.

I bundled into the Robbo with my box of supplies on my lap and as we took off, I left my stomach on the ground. The little helicopter quickly made some height and headed north over the town. The helicopter swayed in the breeze as the wind and rain kept on coming. The view from the sky was more shocking than the view from the water. And even more shocking was the fact that I didn't quite fit into the cockpit, with one leg hanging perilously close to the skid.

It was hard to make out landmarks as we flew over the town. Roughly ninety percent of the town was underwater. There were still people being rescued from their roof tops. In Katherine, there are elevated houses, built on stilts, to catch the breeze and to escape the floods. These were flooded too. The main power station near the river was sparking and the high tensile power lines looked very close to the river. There was no bridge to be seen ... anywhere. The moment I could make out a road, I directed my pilot to my boss's house. She was waiting for me in her front paddock.

I ran over to her with the box. I didn't really have time to talk, as the helicopter had a hundred other jobs to attend to. She asked me if I was going okay. I wished in that moment I could have said... 'yep, goin' steady.' My eyes gave me away. I left her with the supplies and climbed back into the Robbo and back to Katherine East.

CHAPTER 6

WHEN YOUR BEST IS NOT GOOD ENOUGH

The following days in Katherine were a heartbreaking whirl of activity. One of the boarding kennels in town was under water, and the animals had been moved from the kennels to the house to stay dry, when the owners were told to evacuate. Sadly, the house was later inundated and many of the  animals were left to fend for themselves in the floodwater. There were dogs that had gone missing in the evacuation, and some that had fallen out of boats during the rescue attempts. Lots of dogs were straying in the streets, wandering between houses, looking for their owners. I had put an announcement on local radio and so had a number of dogs in my yard, holding them and feeding them until we could find their owners.

Many animals had drowned. Cows were found stuck in trees. Horses shredded their legs on fences in a panic to escape. There were so many animals needing my attention and I didn't have all the medicines and supplies that I needed to help them. It was stressful and overwhelming, to say the least.

One of my patients was a dog that had been clinging to a tree for about two days before he was rescued and brought to my house. His owners were stranded in Darwin, desperate for word about their dog. When we were finally able to connect with my patient's owner over the phone, the news wasn't good.

Bruno was a big Rhodesian Ridgeback. He would have weighed at least 35 kg. He was covered in sores and the skin on his lower limbs was peeling away. His body was riddled with infection, and he was dehydrated and exhausted. I wasn't sure if I was going to be able to save him. His owners were desperate. They knew their house had gone under. They had lost everything. Could I save their dog?

Another patient was a cat that had fallen out of a boat during the rescue attempt, terrified and panicked. It had nearly drowned in the brown, muddy floodwaters as its owners had frantically saved it from the current. The wife wasn't capable of speaking. She had lost everything too. She was in a state of catatonic shock. The husband was trying to hold it all together. Their lives were shattered. Could I save their cat?

Another dog, a rough-looking cattle dog, had been pulled from the floodwaters by its front leg. His owner had heard the sickening snap as his dog was pulled from the water. Now his front leg was broken. His owner looked at me with eyes filled with grief and guilt. Could I help his dog?

Tragically, I was not able to save every animal that came my way in those horrendous couple of weeks. I was able to get Bruno out of Katherine to a clinic in Darwin the moment the highway opened up. A good-hearted soul, queueing in the line to head out of town, willingly became a veterinary ambulance for me, with drip and dog attached and some instructions to take Bruno to a clinic in Darwin when they arrived. Sadly, Bruno struggled on in hospital for nearly two weeks before he passed away. The clinic in Darwin called me later, while I was still processing my disappointment, with the news that Bruno had died from a disease called *melioidosis*. It was fatal. There was nothing I could have done.

The next part of that news, though, was that I had been exposed to melioidosis, and I in turn had exposed my whole household to the disease. It was fatal to humans too. There was an agonising delay between getting that news and the realisation that we were probably going to be okay, based on the lag times of infection and our exposure.

The cat rescued from the floodwater was having trouble breathing and was deteriorating rapidly. I rang for support from colleagues at my old University. I thought there was fluid or pus building up in the chest cavity and I needed to do a chest tap. They talked me through a procedure that I had never done before, with equipment that wasn't quite appropriate, to try and save the cat's life. I gave it my best, but my best wasn't good enough. The cat died in my arms. The wife wailed in despair. The loss was too much for her. I felt the weight of that responsibility and disappointment, and the loss was nearly too much for me too.

As the flood waters receded the bones of the town were exposed - a bit like a carcass torn apart by feral pigs. There was a car in Third Street with prop damage on its roof. Flooded vehicles littered the streets. The mud was deep, and the stench was unbearable.

The clinic was ankle deep in a thick, foetid muddy ooze once the flood waters receded. The dog food that had spilled had fermented and dissipated into the mud, which meant that the mud was even more fragrant in the veterinary clinic than elsewhere. There were a couple of solid days taken up with clearing out shelving and equipment, attempting to salvage and dry some of the clinic contents and hosing everything down. We used a fire hose. It took three attempts before the water we sluiced out came out clear.

It took much longer to count the losses and to start to put some order back into lives that had been ransacked by chaos. Everyone processes their grief differently. Many people had lost everything while others, like me, had been completely spared from any material losses. It seemed unfair, and some people became bitter and resentful in the pain of their loss. People lost loved ones, and many animals were part of that loss. Livestock and livelihoods were also impacted, some businesses went to the wall, and many people became frustrated and angry with their insurance companies. No-one came through that time unscathed.

Within a few weeks of Bruno passing, my client decided to bring a case of negligence against me. She felt that my veterinary care was lacking, and his death was a direct result of my inadequate care. I was inconsolable. I had literally waded through crocodile infested floodwaters to treat him, I had exposed myself and my housemates to a fatal bacterial pathogen and I had arranged for transport to Darwin to continue his care, the very day it became possible to do so.

My boss tried to reassure me that there was no case. Time and time again she repeated her support of my actions and told me that I had done the best I could. But a sinister thought crept into my mind shortly after that legal letter landed on our desk. My best wasn't good enough. I wasn't good enough. I wasn't cut out to be a vet. And all I wanted to do in that moment was run away, as fast and as far as possible.

The next few months I spiralled into a depression. My life was a mess. I had escaped domestic violence, but with not a shred of confidence left. The floods and the letter that followed shattered any self-esteem that remained, the whole episode's sharp edges cutting deep into my soul. My boss could see the spiral. She offered me time off, paid for a hotel in Darwin and offered me a new opportunity to help establish a clinic in a remote coastal location, which she had recently purchased. I agreed to give it a go ... I didn't feel that I could stay in Katherine.

The new clinic was quiet, but it didn't offer me respite from the turmoil in my head. The clinic also had a fairly sketchy history. It had previously been run by people who had been struggling with mental health issues. Drug abuse, alcohol abuse and the tragic death of one of its previous colleagues had led to the purchase. It didn't help me to be rattling around in that lonely space with the ghosts of the past, in a remote location, miles from my family and friends.

I ran away again. This time I spent time on an island, with an old veterinary nursing friend, trying to decompress and recover. I drank too much and none of my problems went away. I decided to take a job in Queensland, packed up my Hilux and left the Northern Territory, only to find that the moment I arrived I felt compelled to leave again.

I decided that the only safe place to go at that time was back home. I didn't feel capable of working. My thoughts and my professional capacity were completely tangled... and like a rag doll cat that had rolled in burrs, it was going to take some time to sort out.

TOXIC AS A SNAKE BITE

I have only ever performed one operation on a snake. It was much more common for me to manage a snake bite than a sick snake, but on this occasion, I had bravely volunteered to treat a snake that was part of a community wildlife and educational display when I was working in the north of Western Australia. My bravery wavered a bit when I arrived to see four pressure bandages lined up on a table beside the snake's enclosure, 'just in case'. The snake I was treating was a King Brown, one of the most dangerous and venomous snakes in that region.

Snake bite in humans and dogs is always an emergency. Pressure is applied to the bite site immediately, to try to constrict the flow of venom through the lymphatic system. Then the patient is rushed to hospital for administration of intravenous anti-venene. Depending on the bite and the amount of venom delivered, multiple vials of antivenene may be required to save the life of the victim.

Australian snakes have three major toxins in their venom. The venom destroys red blood cells and affects the clotting pathway, it can paralyse the patient with neurotoxins, and the venom can also break down muscles. Due to the direct and indirect range of clinical effects of the toxins, all of the major systems of the body are effected. The cardiovascular system can shut down, especially if the heart muscle is affected. The liver and kidneys can go into overdrive and suffer acute damage trying to process the venom and the proteins in the antivenene. So, snake bites can cause catastrophic shut down of every body system and death can come in minutes. The smaller the patient, the more immediate the effects of the venom. Watching and waiting to see if the bite is going to result in toxic effects is just not an option.

(I am happy to say that the King Brown I treated lived to fight another day. He had an abscessed venom gland and the expert handlers that helped me to manage the procedure kept me safe. His abscess was lanced, and he was treated with antibiotics. As a somewhat terrifying addendum to that story, he escaped after the administration of his last dose of antibiotic and slithered away into the suburbs, never to be seen again.... we hope.)

Words can be as toxic as a snake bite. It's always better to process venomous words immediately, but at that time in my life I didn't know how to do that. Watching and waiting seems a ridiculous option, but that is exactly what I did. I watched and waited to see the effects of the trauma I had experienced in the first couple of years working in the outback as a young vet.

I harboured a range of toxic narratives in my soul. Negative words are deadly. Without exception, negative words will kill joy. They have the capacity to destroy your whole operating system. Just like a venom that kills tissues, words have the capacity to destroy confidence, self-esteem, sense of worth, hopes and aspirations. These qualities can all die on the inside. The more you die on the inside, the more hollow you become and the more dreary and dark life becomes.

I found that damaging narratives would run on repeat. They would keep me up at night. They would flood into my consciousness during the day with vivid memories and I would relive the pain. The memories were like a stabbing pain in my side... the pain of the words that had been spoken to me... the pain of the words that I said to myself.

As a teenager, my Mum had walked into my bedroom and saw my father sexually abusing me. In that moment of shock, she said 'you have destroyed my marriage, and I will never forgive you'. I swallowed a toxic cocktail of shame. I blamed myself for my parents' troubled marriage. I believed that there was something intrinsically wrong with me. And I told no-one. Shame kept me silent for years. Rejection entered my heart at that moment. I didn't feel worthy of love. Confronted by my father's dysfunction, my own mother had rejected me. The pain of rejection from a parent or parents is unbearable. We are not designed to cope with such pain.

The words kept circulating.

When I left my first job in outback Western Australia, my boss was disappointed to hear I was leaving, after only six months. He didn't know that I was being stalked by a jilted lover. When he told me I was a disgrace to myself and to my family, I believed those words in that moment. I felt completely disgraced. The words turned over in my head time and time again, like twisting a knife in my side.

Not everything turned out how I wanted it to when I started working in outback Australia. I made mistakes because I was learning and sometimes clients were very disappointed with my inexperienced service.

Clients told me a range of things, including:

'Do you know what you're doing?'
'Are you old enough to be a vet?'
'What did they teach you at vet school?'
'It's your fault my dog is dead.'
'Do you even know how to drive?'
'Don't you know?'
'I want to see the other vet.'
'But you're a girl!'

Most of those comments landed in my heart and were translated into an internal narrative of despair. The words I said to myself were relentless.

'I'm no good.'
'Maybe I wasn't cut out to be a vet.'
'I can't do this.'
'This is too hard.'
'I don't know enough.'
'What was I thinking?'
'Who do you think you are?'
'I am not good enough.'
'I am not enough.'
'I will never be enough.'
'I feel all alone.'
'No-one else has ever experienced what I am going through.'
'I have to figure it out on my own, no-one is going to help me.'
'Everyone will think I am stupid.'
'I am an embarrassment to my profession.'
'I am a failure.'
'I don't deserve better.'
'This is as good as it's ever going to get.'
'I'm just not tough enough.'

Each of these phrases sank into my heart and these words became what I believed about myself. These words sabotaged every hope, dream and aspiration I had when I embarked on my career.

I wanted to run and hide. I wanted all of the pain to go away. I didn't know how to make the words stop.

***

I wanted to erase the first three years of my career as a vet, so my time at home away from work did allow me to refocus my energy on a new direction, a new distraction, a way to continue without losing everything. I decided to try again. This time I needed a better direction, a better plan.

A good percentage of my graduating class from Melbourne University were already living the locum life in England, and they had encouraged me to join them. (A locum is someone who fills a short- or medium-term employment opportunity)

I decided to join my friends from university. In a new country, a new start and the familiarity of my friends from Vet School, I tried desperately to bury my pain and my poisonous thoughts (and words) and do the best I could to live a *normal* life.

PART TWO - UNDIAGNOSED SOUL WOUNDS

NUMBING THE PAIN

Life for me was a painful procedure and alcohol was my anaesthetic. Alcohol addiction is Australia's most socially acceptable vice, and I took my addiction with me to the UK.

My dad was an alcoholic. He was always the life of the party and the last one still drinking. He would keep pressing his friends to have another drink, long after everyone wanted to go to bed and no-one wanted to play cards anymore. Dad would drink when he came home from work to relax and unwind. One beer became two, which became many, every night. Dad drank when he was happy, and he drank when he was sad. Dad drank when he was angry, and he drank when he didn't know what to do.

And he drank to celebrate. From the age of about six or seven, my Dad introduced me to alcohol. First it was a sip from a port glass. Then it became my own glass of wine with dinner on special occasions. By the time I was a teen, my brother and I were

Dad's drinking partners for the birthday celebrations, the Christmas celebrations and any excuse we could find in between.

I was well 'prepared' for university life in the 90's. I stayed in a residential college at Melbourne University where the drinking culture was strongly entrenched. From O Week to exam week, drinking was part of university life.

Once I made it into vet school, the pressure on academic achievement had finally eased, and my drinking became a sport. I was the anchor for the girls' boat-racing team in first year.

I was a regular at the Barn Dance in vet school. I had some notoriety as a competitor in the jelly pit at the Barbarian Feast. In my final year, my study group became the administrators of 'cellars' - the five o'clock wind down drinks on a Friday night. I was never far away if there was a drink on offer.

I was just like my dad. I drank when I was happy. I always drank before I danced. (I danced a lot at uni). I drank when I was sad, because I didn't want to feel sad anymore. I drank because I had a lot of study to do. I drank when I was nervous about exams. I drank to celebrate. It didn't need to be much. Sometimes I would celebrate beating my best friend Jaq at cards. I drank to ease the pain of feeling different. I drank to ease the pain in my soul. I graduated vet school as a highly functioning alcoholic and carried the habit into my working life.

I arrived in the UK and joined my friends in Edinburgh for New Years Eve. We drank in little Scottish pubs; we drank in our backpacker lounges. We travelled, we celebrated the New Year, and we drank some more. Oh, how good it was not to be drinking alone.

CHAPTER 9

DISTRACTION

Travelling to the UK was an amazing adventure. It challenged me in completely new ways, and I was quite convinced that I would be leaving all of my problems on the other side of the world, starting afresh with a clean slate.

Australia and England have a long working relationship, enabling veterinary qualifications obtained in Australia to be recognised in the UK without any further exams or tests.

It was like a breath of fresh air to be living and working with my friends from University. I had graduated from veterinary school in the mid 90's and the class was small. We had spent five years living and working and studying (and partying) together and there were close bonds forged in those years. We had all just gone through the tumultuous experience of exiting the protection of university and entering the workplace, and catching up on the stories breathed life into my soul. I realised I actually wasn't alone. We all had stories of terror and triumph. And there were some great stories.

I settled into a locum position in a town in the Southwest of England. I had one of my best friends living with me in an apartment above the clinic, and another Aussie vet in the apartment next door. We lived and worked together for nearly two years. We could debrief at the end of a long day, sometimes over one or two or six wines. We travelled around England enjoying the opportunity to go hiking or exploring castles and comparing Devonshire teas, when we weren't on call. We talked endlessly about tricky cases, learnt together and journeyed the ups and downs of veterinary life together.

Working in a clinic with six other vets helped to polish some of the rough edges of my veterinary knowledge and techniques, and some even rougher edges of my Australian vernacular, accumulated by osmosis after two and a half years in the outback. I will always remember the kind way my boss would pull me aside and tell me... 'here in England, we would probably prefer you to say it this way...' and give me helpful examples along the way. Sometimes I would remember and get it right...and sometimes I just got it hopelessly wrong.

For example, rabbits are very popular companion animals in England. In Australia, they are the scourge of wildlife, and they are a common pest. In Queensland, it is actually forbidden to keep rabbits as pets. In England, rabbits are vaccinated against myxomatosis. In Australia, we are developing viral diseases like calicivirus to release into the environment to kill rabbits. There is no vaccination for myxomatosis available in Australia. In England, rabbits live a very comfortable life in the lounge room. In Australia, the iconic Akubra hat is made from rabbit pelts.

It was in the context of this cultural difference that I approached my first (and subsequently my last) rabbit consultation at this veterinary clinic. I performed a physical examination to the best of my ability and found the bunny to be in good health. My task was to vaccinate this bunny against myxomatosis. I carefully drew up the vaccination and pinched up some skin at the back of the bunny's neck. I had given hundreds of injections before. This should be no different. But I struggled. I couldn't get the needle through the skin.

And then I muttered under my breath a thought that should have stayed a thought,

'Gosh, rabbits have got tough skin', I said as I used enough force required for the needle to penetrate the skin. And before the client could make any comment... I followed up with 'I guess that's why they make such good hats'.

My boss took me aside later and told me about the tirade that this client had bombarded him with afterwards. Needless to say, he kindly took the rabbit consultations from then on. Regardless of the number of bunnies waiting in the waiting room, none of them came my way!

I was blessed to be part of a good team though, and my learning accelerated beyond my imagination. When I had left Australia to work in England, it was my goal to work and save as much as possible, come back to Australia, buy some land and leave the veterinary industry forever. It had taken just three short years of working as a vet for me to conclude that I simply wasn't cut out for the profession. But then, after spending just over eighteen months in a privately owned group practice—with a supportive team and a delightful boss—I began to reconsider. Perhaps I didn't have to leave veterinary work after all.

CHAPTER 10

PERFORMANCE IN CAREER

Feeling more settled in my working life was a blessed relief. But it was strangely unsatisfying. I had anticipated feeling a great sense of inner achievement and satisfaction as I started to feel a little more accomplished in my career. I had hoped against hope that at some point I wouldn't wake up with a writhing mass of butterflies in my stomach in anticipation of the day's caseload. Perhaps, after three short years, it was time to find my passion in a specialty field or improve my skills in a certain area.

Working in the outback had brought me into close proximity with Australia's amazing wildlife, and I was especially fond of birds of prey. In my first job in Newman, I had worked with wedge tailed eagles. I was fascinated by their form and power and also somewhat terrified by their grip force. (The grip force of a wedge tailed eagle is no less than 400 pounds per square inch.)

In England, I had the opportunity to learn falconry. In medieval times, this was a form of hunting where birds would be trained to fly and capture prey and return to their handler. I enrolled in a beginner's course to understand more and to experience the feeling of a bird of prey flying onto my gloved fist. It was an incredibly special experience. Maybe I would be able to use this skill to work in wildlife rehabilitation back home in Australia?

I also explored another opportunity that satisfied the inner child in me who had spent a lifetime reading the books of Gerald Durrell. I visited the Jersey Wildlife Conservation Trust and enrolled in a twelve-week Diploma in Endangered Species Management. I had the extraordinary privilege of working with students from all around the world, each with a unique perspective on wildlife.

I was shocked to hear that some of the rangers from Africa had been threatened at gun point by poachers. There was a beautiful quiet soul from Sri Lanka who had spent hours upon hours in the rainforest, studying a small critically endangered (but otherwise nondescript) brown bird. Most of the other students were already working in the field of wildlife and brought amazing stories and experiences to the group.

For twelve whole weeks I was able to indulge myself in the world of wildlife management, and I tried to get my head around the state of the global environment and the threatening processes that endanger wildlife. In a very sobering workshop, our group got to discuss a hypothetical problem based in West Africa. Our tutors described a scenario where there was a critically endangered monkey that was being eaten by the local people as a prized bush food. Never in my life have I felt so humbled by the discussion.

My mind was racing through strategies that could be employed to stop the people from eating the monkeys and my African brothers were discussing what right do we have to determine if a man feeds his family or not. The stark reality of poverty was not part of my calculation. Sitting there in that class, it began to dawn on me that the process of endangerment would never be solved where there were whole people groups, nations even, that were eating wildlife as a critical protein source.

Wildlife problems in Australia seemed so much more straightforward. Yes, there was habitat loss, there was predation by feral species (including cats and foxes and wild dogs), and there were invasive weeds. But we did not have to worry about subsistence hunting. Yet, Australia has an atrocious record of species extinctions.

My foray into wildlife management study was depressingly short-lived. After realising that it took more than a million GB pounds to rehabilitate a golden lion tamarind in the rainforest of Brazil and that people all around the world didn't have enough to eat, I came to the conclusion that there were infinite complexities involved. Not only did these make my brain hurt, but I also realised that wildlife was not always the priority where people lived in poverty. At last count, roughly half of the global population lives in poverty. Wildlife endangerment is a first world problem.

While I was starting to wonder what other area of expertise I could sink my teeth into, I was invited to participate in an incredible opportunity. A rather eclectic study group comprising of vets and dentists from Australia and the USA was taking a trip to Ecuador and the Galapagos Islands. I didn't imagine that this trip would somehow qualify me for a career change, but I jumped at the chance.

CHAPTER 11

TRAVEL AND ADVENTURE

Maybe travel was the next passion to explore?!!

The trip was so amazing that even now it's hard to describe. I booked a side excursion into the Amazon rainforest and was joined by one of my colleagues from the tour who was up for some more adventure.
Our tour was cut short, inconveniently, by a volcano that was erupting in Ecuador. Apparently, ash from exploding volcanoes fouls up jet engines. I was impatient and couldn't bear to wait... but we had no choice. We bravely signed up for the first flight entering the country and climbed onboard without a second thought. Those second thoughts only came when we were in the air. It was without a doubt the most terrifying flight of my life.

The pilot of our flight from Miami to Quito finally landed after what was the most turbulent ride I had ever experienced. On our approach to landing, the turbulence was so bad that the cabin overhead lockers were springing open. After a lot of Spanish shouting, there were tears of joy when we touched down. The whole plane gave the pilot a resounding ovation with cheers and loud clapping.

We disembarked past soldiers with AK47's and spent the night in Quito before catching a light airplane into the jungle. I had experienced a lot of light aircraft flights in my job in the outback when we had to fly to various stations to prepare cattle for export. I thought I was a veteran of the light aircraft. Maybe it's the language barrier that makes it more anxiety inducing. We had flown over hours of thick, impenetrable rainforest, when the plane started to circle. The pilot continued to circle our runway for a couple of minutes before he had the okay to land. I didn't think there was anyone in sight. What could possibly be causing the delay?

It was only as we landed that I realised the dilemma. The runway wasn't sealed. And it consisted of thick, sticky mud. The plane initially touched down smoothly but then lurched to a sudden stop in ankle deep mud. From there we picked our way down a treacherous slope to a river tributary where a very long, skinny boat awaited us.

There were just a handful of tourists with me and the colleague from my tour group. We made our way down the river to our accommodation which was little jungle cabins on stilts over a backwater of the Pastaza River. We had several days of exploring the jungle with a local Amazonian Indian guide. We saw three-toed sloths, pink river dolphins, macaws, toucans and howler monkeys. We saw capybara and cayman alligators in the twilight and dusk. We trekked through the jungle and saw beautiful butterflies, leaf cutter ants and a kaleidoscope of tiny poison dart frogs. We even happened across the footprints of a jaguar, so fresh that we could see the pores in his foot pads. We didn't spot him, but no doubt he had eyes on us.

From the beauty and humid chaos of the jungle we made our way back to Quito to join our study group and start the tour. The travel highlights continued unabated. We had conferences with wildlife rangers in Ecuador and learnt about the threats to wildlife. We visited one of Ecuador's foremost zoos as well as a ranch out of town. From there we flew to the Galapagos Islands. It was like stepping into a National Geographic wildlife documentary. We shared beaches with sea lions, explored rock pools peppered with Sally Lightfoot crabs and marine iguanas, swam with penguins and hiked up volcanoes, past lazy land iguanas. We even had foot races with giant Galapagos tortoises ... no guesses who won there!

I was so captivated by the Galapagos that I decided to abandon the study tour and stay on the island for as long as my visa would permit. I said farewell to my new-found friends and colleagues and made my way back to the town of Puerta Ayora, found some cheap accommodation and booked in for some scuba diving.

I spent the next three weeks in a state of extreme bliss. I dived some of the coldest but most beautiful waters on the planet. I watched schooling hammerhead sharks, marvelled at manta rays so large that they blocked out the sun. I watched the liquid movement and beauty of sea lions underwater. I could gaze upon tropical fish and stunning underwater seascapes for as long as my tank of air would allow. In the evenings, I would join up with other dive buddies and fellow travellers to eat fresh seafood and talk about the day's diving.

After my dive package ran out, I jumped onboard a sailing vessel and explored more of the islands. I snorkelled, hiked and explored as much of the Galapagos as I could manage. It was truly devastating when my visa expired and I had to make my way back to reality and the mainland. Immersed in the beauty of the Galapagos, my soul had experienced a kind of peace and tranquillity that I had never experienced before.

Back in Quito, I had a couple of days to regroup and plan the next phase of my travel adventure in the USA. I was sad to leave Ecuador, but excited for the challenge of navigating the USA with just a tent and my sleeping bag, a little hire car and a map book of the best national parks in the country.

DANGER (RISK TAKING)

I didn't intentionally embark on a tour of risk and personal endangerment in the USA, but that is pretty much what transpired. I was incredibly naive when I began my travel in the States. Perhaps it was my naivety that saved me time and time again. My plan was to visit as many national parks and natural wonders as I could in eight weeks. I was on a budget and planned to camp my way around the southern states. It was not long before I found a flaw in that plan.

Having come off the back of such a beautiful time with complete strangers in South America, I was becoming bolder and more confident about my personal safety. And it was not long before I found myself in a very sticky situation.

I had made my way from Miami to the Florida panhandle and the everglades. I was excited to explore the wildlife in this region and made my way to a national parks office to book in a bird-watching tour, scheduled for dawn the next morning. With an evening to fill in, I found a campground and set up my tent and made my way to the pub next door to enjoy a meal and a few Budweisers to end the day.

I was sitting at the bar, the same way I had sat at the bar in outback Western Australia, and was approached by two men. Within seconds, I realised that this was not the wisest move. I had a very sensitive nose for sleazy men and sniffed danger in a heartbeat with these two. I suddenly felt very alone.

The guy sitting next to me launched into his line...

'Have you met any American men in your travels?' I eyed this guy and felt his intimidation in an instant.

'No... and I am not really intending to,' I said, trying to feel brave.

'Well, honey, you may not want to meet any American men... but we might just meet with you later,' the guy sneered.

This sounded to me like a direct threat of sexual violence. I immediately thought of my tent, pitched barely a hundred metres away and realised I had nowhere to run, nowhere to hide. Summoning up my best Aussie accent and tone of dry derision, I replied.

'Mate, you scare me' - said with as much bravado and sarcasm as I could muster. I then turned back to my beer and took a hearty swig.

It was like one of those moments in an old Western, when the piano player stops and the bar goes silent. The guy slammed down his beer and stalked out of the pub with his buddy. In that space of awkward stillness, a group of young people approached me from across the room. They were keen to introduce themselves.

'We've never seen Bob put down like that before!' they exclaimed. 'Where are you from?'

I was keen for company and so we struck up a conversation, and once again I was in the safety of 'stranger-friends' and felt much more relaxed.

One of the girls asked me a simple question. 'Do you like to party?' To me, at that time in my life, 'party' meant having a few beers and dancing.

'Sure,' I said with enthusiasm.

'OK then, let's go!'

Within seconds I was in the back of a car with four others, sandwiched in the middle of the back seat.

'We've got a few stops to make,' the driver turned and told to me.

'Okay, sure...,' I said, wondering what I had gotten myself into.

At the first stop, the guy in the passenger seat jumped out and everyone else stayed put in the car. I was starting to feel the effects of adrenaline and too much beer, and I wondered vaguely what was going on.

Our mate came back with something in his hand. 'Here,' he said to me. 'Hold this'.

I opened up my hand and took a hold of a rock. Well, at first it appeared to be a rock, but it was white and crystalline.

'You can tell it's the good Columbian stuff, because of the hint of yellow,' my newfound friend told me, as my eyes widened.

In that moment I realised I was holding a goodly quantity of cocaine.

At the next stop, there was a large quantity of marijuana purchased, and we headed back to 'party'. I was so far out of my depth that I was on the verge of panic. Only the alcohol in my system and a strong survival instinct which demanded that I stay cool, kept me on track. We had driven for an indeterminable amount of time, in the dark, on roads I didn't know, in a car with people I only had known for ten minutes, to an unknown destination. I had no idea what to do next.

We piled out of the car into a small house with a grubby living room. There was a guy lounging in an old sofa with dubious springs, slumped and barely awake. There were beer bottles on the coffee table and the ground. He had tattoos from his neck down, covering the entirety of his body.

My new buddies laid out their haul of contraband and started doing lines of cocaine. They encouraged me to do some lines too, but I quickly started making excuses.

'I have never done this before, and I don't want to waste your money'.

They insisted time and time again. Reluctantly I took a crumb from the table on the tip of my finger and popped it in my mouth. It was bitter and the effects were immediate. Turns out that cocaine is a local anaesthetic. My tongue became numb, my speech was slurred, and I was oddly excited for the future, despite the immediate concern I had of returning to my tent.

The guy on the sofa gazed in my direction and smiled.

'You don't belong here,' he said to me. 'Would you like a lift home?' he offered, as he finished yet another beer.

I could barely believe my ears and without wanting to seem too eager, I replied, 'yes, please', like a silly schoolgirl after detention.

I climbed into a rusty old pickup truck with the guy, whose name was Hank. He was on parole and had been out of prison for barely a month. He was working as a deck hand on a fishing boat and was ready to start work in a few hours' time. I didn't spend much time contemplating whether he was sober enough to drive, the alternative of staying with my new buddies being way less attractive. Hank and I chatted about mullet and the everglades and the drug trade for the rest of the time it took us to get back to the pub. The pub was shut, there were no vehicles in sight, except for my lonely tent and my hire car. With a rush of adrenaline, I remembered Bob and his sinister threat from earlier in the night. It felt like a lifetime ago now, but my heart wouldn't settle.

Hank looked at me and asked if I would be okay. I sincerely hoped I would be. It was 3.30 am and there was no movement in the area. Everyone had gone home and gone to bed. I thanked Hank again for the lift and waved as he drove off. I could barely believe my luck. I was back at my tent, nothing had been stolen or ransacked, and I was safe and alive, and maybe a little more worldly wise than I had been six hours ago.

I climbed into my tent and snuggled into my sleeping bag. I stared at the roof until first light, listening intently for a car, footsteps, or any other sign of life. I was ready to make a beeline for my car and lock myself in it if I needed to. But no threat came and as the darkness of the night faded, I packed up my tent and drove my car to the National Parks office and parked in their carpark, waiting for the office to open and my birdwatching tour to begin.

As I sat in that boat, learning about the everglades and the magnificent wetland ecosystem, I added a new narrative to my self-condemning internal dialogue.

'How could I be so stupid and still breathe?'

The tour finished, and I mapped out a course to the nearest trailer park, where I camped amongst a community of retirees in Winnebagos and took some time to regroup.

I learnt a lot during my eight weeks touring the USA with a car and a tent. I discovered that Apalachicola State Reserve on New Years Eve can be a rowdy place, especially when the majority of my fellow campers belonged to the Racoon Shooters Club of Panhandle Florida. It was yet another night that I spent staring at the roof of my tent, as the gunfire continued sporadically into the night to celebrate the coming of another year.

I learnt that not every invitation to check out someone's camper van is as innocent as it may seem.

I learnt that the highway patrol in the USA is very particular about where you have your hands when they pull you over for a routine check. I definitely didn't get that one right. I was fumbling in all sorts of locations for documentation and licence and passport, which elevated my patrolman's blood pressure to a level that was nearly catastrophic. I later discovered that most policemen expect you to have a concealed weapon or gun somewhere. And tragically, there had been a recent fatality in the police force when a highway patrolman had been shot dead by a driver caught for speeding.

I learnt that most people expect you to have a gun. One man asked me if I had a piece. I had no idea what a piece was. My mind raced - piece of pie? Piece of cake - in Australia that's slang for 'easy done'...what did he mean? And when I asked further, he explained that I should be carrying a gun for my own safety.

I also learnt not to judge people by their appearances. At the end of my time in the US, I had arranged to do some dive training in Marathon, Florida and camped at a caravan park nearby. It just so happened that I camped next to a group of bikies from Philadelphia. Initially they wondered out loud, in a somewhat intimidating way, whether I would stay in that location. In that moment, I had a decision to make. Fight or flight? Or conversation? Again, mustering up the best Aussie accent I could, I grabbed a six pack of beer and said 'G'day, how're you goin'?' to four muscled-up, tattooed Harley Davidson riding bikers. I introduced myself to them and they were pretty excited to learn about Australia and had a million questions about Crocodile Dundee and whether there were kangaroos skipping down the main street. I had a blast. From that afternoon on, for the rest of my time in Marathon, I felt safe, included and protected, in a way I had never felt before. For a brief week I became an honorary rider with the boys from Philadelphia, and I learnt never again to judge someone based on appearances.

I also learnt that you can safely navigate around the USA with a car and a tent and no gun and have a fantastic time.

After that trip, I caught the travel bug. I mingled work with travel to see if I could scratch the growing itch in my soul. I went scuba diving in the Red Sea. I travelled to Ireland and around Scotland. Hot off my experience at Jersey Zoo, I decided that the next step was to travel with a mission or cause. I investigated a group called Coral Cay Conservation and signed up for a six-week volunteering experience in Honduras, mapping the reef and helping the local people develop a sustainable tourism dive industry, as an alternative to fishing with explosives or cyanide. And I felt good about myself, for a moment. Maybe this would bring satisfaction and fulfilment, and the peace and rest I so desperately desired.

Diving in Honduras was amazing. I learnt all about the different reef fish and corals, I learnt to tie one-handed bowline knots underwater, I learnt to manage conservation mapping and documentation while I was diving, and I loved it. I loved it all, all except the sandflies ... and except for the moment when I descended too quickly and realised instantly that I had a problem with my eardrum.

The team at Coral Cay Conservation were well prepared. There was a nurse on staff, and she was able to assess that my ears were inflamed and swollen. There was not much that they could do, though, so I decided to wait it out and see if my ear would improve, taking the Nurofen that I had packed in my emergency medical kit.

One week later, with little to no resolution in my ear, a great deal of discomfort and an alarming amount of hearing loss, I decided to seek medical help in Honduras. The team at CCC took me by boat to the nearest bus-stop and I had a staff member travel with me to the nearest hospital. The bus trip was rough, hot and unpleasant but I knew I needed help.

I arrived at the hospital and have never felt so lost and alone. The hospital was a rammed earth building with a dirt floor. There was a mark on the wall indicating rising damp and there were dogs, pigs and chickens wandering through reception. A large number of mums with new babies were waiting in reception, and most of the babies were crying. A single ceiling fan was wobbling its way around and around, barely disturbing the thick tropical air. It was hot and sticky and uncomfortable, and a perfect breeding ground for bacteria, I said to myself as I approached reception. I spoke very rudimentary Spanish. The staff at the hospital spoke very little English. However, I spoke enough Spanish mingled with sign language to convey my problem to the reception staff and they ushered me down the corridor to the emergency department.

I tried to protest and tell them that it wasn't an emergency, but they insisted that I wait in the hallway, facing the door to the ER. Alone with my thoughts I took a look around the room. There was a long line of people waiting to see the doctor. Some people looked in pretty bad shape. One man had a head injury, and I could see blood staining the bandages on his head. Another lady was doubled over in pain, making soft groaning sounds to herself.

After a relatively short period of time, a tired doctor emerged and called me in. I looked around at the others in the hallway and tried to gesticulate that they should be seen first. The emergency doctor shook her head and said in a thick accent, 'come in.'

I repeated my most practised line of Spanish - namely that I don't speak much Spanish, and the emergency doctor smiled and said, 'but I do speak a little English.' It was an enormous relief. I explained my situation. I suspected that I had suffered a diving injury and perhaps had ruptured my eardrum. Our poor communication was compounded by the fact that my hearing was poor, but eventually I understood that I was to go with the doctor.

I started to become anxious. I didn't want to be admitted, and I didn't understand why we had to walk back out of the consultation area into the hospital corridor. My doctor gently grasped my arm and walked me into another consultation room. To my horror there was already someone in that room. It was a mum and her baby, and the medical team were conducting a gynaecological exam. I didn't know where to look, so I hastily fixed my eyes to the floor. My doctor manoeuvred me to a wall where I glanced up to spot an otoscope. An otoscope is a simple instrument that looks into ears. Every veterinary clinic in Australia would have one in every consultation room and perhaps multiple spares in the treatment area. In this hospital in Honduras there was only one.

The doctor looked into my bad ear first. The pain as she plunged the scope into my ear canal was toe curling. I wasn't sure if there was infection or just inflammation but, in that moment, I understood why dogs will often resist or even try to bite their vet when we perform an ear exam. They hurt.

The doctor withdrew the otoscope and turned my head to look in the other ear. I was instantly worried about cross contamination. I didn't want that scope in my good ear without being cleaned, especially if I had an infection in my other ear. I refused examination on my other ear and the doctor became extremely frustrated with me. We returned to the emergency department consultation room, and she stared at me from across the desk.

'You need a surgery', she told me.

'Please no surgery', I said perhaps a little too quickly.

'You have blood in your middle ear, and I need to release the pressure' the doctor said, drawing me a picture on a notepad as she explained the problem.

I looked around that hospital room, with a dirt floor and rammed earth walls and compared it to the stark, sterile environment of the veterinary hospitals I had worked in. I couldn't consent to surgery in this hospital. I felt sick to the pit of my stomach. This was the main hospital for the whole region. There was one otoscope in the building. Did they even have a gaseous anaesthetic machine, I wondered? I felt so embarrassed at the inequity I experienced in that emergency department that day as urgent cases waited for me to clumsily convey my refusal for surgery. I asked for an insurance certificate. I had travel insurance, and I knew I would need some documentation. The doctor scribbled something in Spanish on a small prescription pad and gave it to me. I tried to thank her for her time, but she sighed and rubbed her head and waved me out the door with a deep sense of frustration. Frustration and exhaustion don't have language barriers. Her tired body did the talking.

I was disappointed that I couldn't go diving - a first world problem. I was worried about my ear and anxious because of the pain and terrified that I had done some permanent damage to my hearing. I was also doubting myself. Could I trust that doctor to operate on my ear? I knew there was no point staying in Honduras for another month because I couldn't contribute much to the project. Would it be okay for me to fly?

What had started as a great plan to contribute my skills and energy to marine conservation and redistribute wealth and resources to people who really needed it, became a hasty retreat when the going got tough. Once again, I felt like I didn't have what it takes. I was incredibly hard on myself and deeply disappointed and I returned to England with my tail between my legs.

DYSFUNCTION (WALKING WITH A LIMP)

While adventuring around the world as a young professional person with the world at my feet, I became aware that I had a problem. I couldn't really define my problem; indeed, it was much easier to deny or ignore it. Again and again, I found myself wondering what life was all about. I was mostly unhappy and never fully satisfied. I had experienced incredible opportunities through travel and my career, and yet, I couldn't shake the feeling that something was still missing.

I was walking with a limp.

Walking with a limp is tiring. It puts strain on lots of other parts of your body and leads to compensatory muscle soreness. If it's severe and chronic enough, you might need to use crutches to carry you through. Alcohol was always my crutch of choice, but it never quite dulled the pain enough.

Denying that you have a problem is much easier than ignoring it. Denial is all about trying to convince yourself that life is under control and that you are the master of your own destiny. Denial means your problem is sitting in your blind spot. At the first hint of awareness, you immediately paint over it with colourful, glossy paint and shift focus to your pretty, polished picture.

Ignoring your problem is harder. You are aware that you have a problem, even though you can't pinpoint exactly what it is. Sometimes, the easiest way to realise you have a problem is when a range of different people start asking, "What's your problem?"

I had so many problems that denial was no longer a realistic strategy. Knowing that I had many problems didn't help either. I never knew which one to focus on, and I could never really define exactly what my problem was. The truth was, I was carrying a whole swag of unruly emotions and erratic behaviours that had a habit of erupting at the most awkward and embarrassing moments—and I had little control over any of them.

My life began to feel like I was trying to keep a beach ball underwater; I didn't want anyone to notice that I was struggling. Keeping a beach ball underwater requires amazing balance and concentration and it is exhausting. It's not a sustainable way to do life.

I had tried so many things. Thinking that a change of career would be the answer, I had been about to step away from veterinary science into a lifetime of diving and marine conservation when my body let me down and my ear injury excluded that possibility as a career option.

I had met a lovely guy in the UK who was truly a fun-loving and generous soul. He had invited me into his life and community in the most beautiful of ways and had restored my faith in the possibility of having a relationship in the future. But I just couldn't commit. I struggled to let anyone get too close, because relationships were too difficult.

I had worked in a great veterinary practice, surrounded by friends and earned a great income. I learnt new skills and developed confidence along the way, but still I felt empty.

Maybe I was just homesick? Maybe it was time to return home. Maybe I would find the answers to the emptiness I was feeling back under the harsh Australian sunshine with my feet planted in red dirt.

CHAPTER 14

DISABLEMENT (AVOIDANCE AND AMPUTATION)

Transition to life back in Australia took me nearly twelve months. It took me nearly that long to say no to the marriage proposal I had left hanging in Essex and the same amount of time to decide where in Australia I wanted to live. I worked in locum  positions in the Northern Territory again and found delight behind the wheel of my Hilux, driving vast distances from my home in Victoria to get there. I also tried a job on the South Coast of New South Wales, while recommencing study, this time in Wildlife Health at the University of Sydney.

This time I was trying a new strategy - avoidance. Avoidance is like amputation. It means trying to exclude all the things in your life that are painful. You cut away the damaged bits of your life and make do with what you have left. Amputation is like walking with a limp, but it's more severe and permanent. There are enormous stresses on the rest of the body with an amputation.

Relationships seemed to cause an unending amount of pain in my life. I had experienced a range of extremely negative relationships and one really positive one, but both were painful. Maybe I would be better off living a single life, and cut out relationships altogether?

I still wasn't sure if veterinary science was my problem. I had entered into a love-hate relationship with my career. I found the constant interaction with people a huge drain on my emotional strength. I often couldn't distinguish whether my client's comments were professional preferences or personal attacks. The emotional rollercoaster of working with people every day was huge. I was determined, as much as I could, to eliminate people from my life. I thought a career in extensive wildlife management in a remote location would be my next dream job and I was figuring out a way to get there. Cutting out the grind of a service-based caring career was the next step.

And I missed the outback, like an ache in my heart. The only place I really found peace in my life was driving a straight road to the horizon under the vault of a deep blue sky, through a red dirt desert. So, I took a job in Broome, a remote country town in the Kimberley region of Western Australia and drove on as many dirt roads as I could, to get there.

CHAPTER 15

THE DAMAGE OF A MISDIAGNOSIS

What I didn't realise at the time was the damage caused by a misdiagnosis. Having a wounded soul and not being able to define or address the problem is like having cancer while ignoring the niggling pain or the symptoms that say that something is not quite right. And also throwing the reminder for a screening test in the bin for several years in a row. You can't treat what you can't see, and you can't see the problem if you don't ask for help. And just like cancer, a soul wound can spread into every facet of your life.

I had been misdiagnosing my pain for years. I knew I had lived through many traumatic experiences, but I hadn't ever sought any meaningful help to process them. I had no idea that the trauma of my childhood had led to the pain and trauma I later experienced in my relationships. Or that it made relationships a near impossibility. I didn't associate my childhood abuse with my dislike of male bosses, or my utter disrespect for authority. My attitude to men in general was at best distrustful, which made working with male colleagues extremely challenging. I barely understood why I was afraid of failure and so desperate for validation in my work life and my career. I couldn't connect the dots. I had been floundering in life since childhood, but had paradoxically achieved enough success in my career and in my profession to mask my dysfunction, even from myself at times.

But over time, the misdiagnosis became catastrophic. Like a cancer of the soul, my erratic behaviour and volatile emotions spread to nearly every part of my life.

I was having trouble at work. I couldn't manage people very well, especially emotional clients. I struggled with conversations that were difficult and would avoid them in unprofessional ways. I struggled with elements of my job that are unavoidable. Euthanasia of pets took a huge toll on my soul. I was distracted and I suffered from brain fog. I would often leave tasks unfinished. I couldn't handle criticism or correction. I didn't have one performance review in Broome without bursting into tears. My boss didn't really know what to do with me.

My physical health also began to suffer. I had developed hypothyroidism in my early twenties, but my medication and supplementation had been inconsistent and piecemeal. I lived in a permanent energy deficit, that was propped up with caffeine. I had a terrible diet and a range of gut complaints. I had an unhealthy obsession with food, diet and exercise and weight fluctuations that were incredibly hard to keep on top of. I didn't like myself, and I didn't like my life.

CHAPTER 16

LOVE SUBSTITUTION

One day, standing at the front counter of the veterinary clinic in Broome, I said out loud, 'I think I am ready for a dog again and I would like a tan staffy with a black nose'. My heart had been broken by losing a puppy five long years ago when I had started work in Newman. I had fallen in love with a  border collie puppy that I later diagnosed as having a heart defect. Shelby's life was short, but I loved her so deeply. I lost her when she was just six months old, and it took a long time for my heart to heal—longer still to reach the place where I felt ready to try again… to love again.

Within three days a stranger walked into the clinic off the street with a little puppy in their hands.

'I found this little one on the road - she's not in good shape and you might have to put her down', the guy said as he handed her over and walked back out of the clinic without so much as a goodbye.

I took the little puppy and looked her over. She was a stray. We were obliged to keep her for a few days to see if anyone would claim her. She was barely five weeks old. Her ears were full of dog ticks, and her belly was hard and round with worms and she was just skin and bone. And she was a tan staffy-looking dog with a black nose. I knew she was mine.

I spent the next hour picking the ticks off this little puppy, gave her some worming paste and decided that if she made it through the night, I would keep her. I named her Kirby, (because she was found on the curb) and she became the most loyal, loving dog you could ever hope for. She showed me what unconditional love looks like. Every day, it was her delight to show me love, like it was the most exciting thing in the world to do. When I got home from work, she would greet me as if she hadn't seen me for days. She gave me the love I so desperately needed at the lowest ebb of my life. It was like a critical infusion of love at a time when I had nearly haemorrhaged out.

Kirby came everywhere with me. She would come to work with me and hang out the back, waiting for a moment to play. In our lunch break we would run on Cable Beach and swim in the ocean. At home after work she would sometimes be allowed inside to sit and watch TV with me… but always on her mat. But, occasionally, at the end of the week, I would relent, and she would spoon with me on the lounge as we watched a movie. She was so full of life, it was impossible to ignore her.

Kirby provided me with love when the rest of the world seemed unlovely. The world was unlovely to me because I had been hurt by people close to me, and I had experienced a counterfeit love, one rooted in control and manipulation. Love isn't always pure. I had experienced love with conditions, or a transactional kind of love. I had been hurt over and over again, and my heart was hardened. It was really difficult for me to receive love, and I struggled to trust the process—and to embrace the vulnerability that comes with loving others.

But love was as vital to my life as the blood in my veins. I couldn't survive without love; I was critically 'love anaemic'. One of my surgery lecturers used to say, 'the bleeding always stops when the blood pressure is low enough'. I had almost haemorrhaged love and trust to the point of death, and my love tank was completely dry. I had become loveless. Kirby was like a life-saving emergency bolus of intravenous love. Kirby supported me through my critical love deficit. Her love licked my broken pieces back together again.

PART THREE - HEALING OF A WOUNDED SOUL

WE ARE WOUNDED IN ISOLATION,
BUT HEAL IN COMMUNITY.

CHAPTER 17

RAIN IN THE DESERT

While I was living and working in Broome, I found a community. And while I was enjoying doing life with a great group of people, I met a man who would change the trajectory of my life. There was something very different about him, a quality I couldn't put my finger on, and it was intoxicating and intriguing.

We met at a charity event held in Broome called the Rotary Pentathlon. The Pentathlon comprised of a series of social sporting events including golf, tennis, lawn bowls, pool and darts. It was a fundraising event for the local Rotary club. To enter the pentathlon, you needed a team of two, so I teamed up with my buddy Cath. It was a fancy dress event, and the team needed a theme. We decided to dress up as wallflowers and raided the local op shops (charity stores) for vaguely matching bridesmaids' dresses. We paired the dresses with ugly fake teeth and wore horn-rimmed glasses and wore our hair in plaits.

LINDY PRICE

The first event of the Pentathlon was a Calcutta at the pub. In the Calcutta, the teams were paraded on stage and auctioned off to the highest bidder in the same way you might place a bet on a horse race. To increase the bidding, (by holding a longer stage time) some teams would do a short performance or a skit. If, at the end of the Pentathlon, your team came through with a win, you would receive a cash prize. Ultimately the Calcutta was designed to raise funds for the children's ward at Broome hospital, so the monetary rewards were not great, but the rivalry was fierce.

My friend Cath was a pretty handy singer, so in keeping with our theme as shy wallflowers, she sang a Kasey Chambers song titled, 'Am I not pretty enough', while I did interpretive dance. I think it's best if I say as little as possible about the quality of that performance, except that Cath was a pretty good singer! I am not a huge fan of fancy dress, but that night in my wallflower costume, I felt bold. I spotted a young man dressed up as a cowboy… and on that first night, as Cath and I exited the stage, I brushed past him and whispered in his ear, 'I do like a good-looking cowboy.'

So, for the next five days, starting with the golf event on the Sunday afternoon and then proceeding through each night of the week following, the Pentathlon unfolded. Cath and I were both outrageously competitive and we fancied our prospects in the all-female overall teams event. So, we took it as seriously as one can, with billy bob buck teeth and your hair in plaits. All the while, I had my eye on the cowboy. And as is often the case in a small country town, everyone noticed that I had my eye on the cowboy. By the end of the week, my subtle advances and the cowboy's subtle reciprocation were noticed, and the organisers of the event held a mock wedding at the final night's celebration.

It was all good fun until the costumes came off, and we then had to figure out if there was something worth pursuing underneath. As it turned out, we both headed out in different directions for nearly a month before we had that first date. The second and third dates followed hot on the heels of the first date and by the end of that weekend, we were a couple.

My cowboy's name was Mal. He was fun-loving, intelligent, sporty and adventurous. He had a degree in construction management and was currently working in Broome as a self-employed builder. He loved camping and four-wheel driving and exploring the outback and he was well travelled, both in Australia and overseas. He had a love for music and the arts and was cultured in ways I didn't expect to find in a man in Broome.

The first time I went camping with Mal, we went north along the Dampier Peninsula to a place called Price's Point. I camped in my swag in the back of my Hilux like I usually did, but I woke in the morning to a very pleasant surprise. Mal was up and was stoking our campfire and asked me if I would like bacon and eggs and a cappuccino for breakfast. In that moment I knew this was the man for me!

The next nine months went by in a whirlwind of bliss for me. I rediscovered joy as I got to know Mal. As I spent time with him, parts of my heart that I thought were dead, or at least dormant, started coming back to life. Like rain in the desert, the dryness of my life was transforming into something beautiful, with life and colour and noise. We started dreaming of what our future together might look like. At some point I moved in with Mal. At the time it seemed to make sense. And quite importantly, Kirby liked Mal and Mal liked Kirby, so we formed a little family and started to do life together.

One afternoon, as we sat in Mal's house on his day bed, pondering our future, we started talking about a five-year plan. What do we want in the next five years? It was a confronting moment. I had never planned five years ahead. To be honest I had only ever planned travel destinations. I had never contemplated what I wanted in life, and I was already thirty years old. Without too much thought and knowing that my internal biological clock was ticking, I said out loud, 'I think I would like two kids in the next five years.'

Mal was thoughtful in that moment.

'What about marriage?' he asked.

The marriage question was a tricky one for me. I had seen my parents unhappily married, for the greater part of my childhood. My Dad's alcohol addiction and my Mum's unspoken dysfunction created a toxic atmosphere for us as kids. They would always have their arguments when we went to bed, hoping that we wouldn't be listening. My brother and I were always listening. In my experience marriage wasn't happy.

And then there were my own experiences of relationships. The first serious relationship I had started when I was leaving Newman. It was toxic and abusive for eighteen months and culminated in a marriage proposal. When I finally plucked up the courage to say 'no', my engagement ring was flung into the bush, and I was punished financially for months to come.

The second relationship was more positive. It too, had culminated in a marriage proposal, but somewhere deep in my heart I couldn't commit, and I left that relationship knowing I had caused disappointment and pain.

The third relationship I experienced was completely positive, but I couldn't marry an Englishman. I knew that I would spend my life homesick for Australia's sunshine and wide-open spaces, and we couldn't find a compromise that felt right in my heart. That relationship ended and I knew that my fear of commitment and flakiness had been the cause of a heartache that lasted for months. Every marriage proposal I had received signalled a painful end to the relationship.

To be completely fair, I was afraid of marriage because I equated it with pain, and I really didn't want Mal to propose. I believed that I had had three strikes, and I was out. But I did want to commit to Mal, and I did want to spend the rest of my life with him. At the time, I told myself that marriage was an expensive formality that I didn't want to risk.

So, we talked about kids. My Mum had struggled for years to conceive my brother and me. I had also had my own share of reproductive dysfunction, as a result of hypothyroidism. I didn't anticipate that falling pregnant would be easy for me. Truthfully, I expected it would take years. So together Mal and I agreed to start trying for a kid and I came off my contraceptive pill.

One month later I was pregnant! Mal was so shocked when he heard the news that he sanded straight over his arm that day on the building site. Lucky for him that he was sanding, not using a drop saw that day. The next nine months were a very sobering time for us both. In order to safeguard my baby's health, I had cut down drastically on my drinking. The combination of the sudden withdrawal of my self-prescribed 'emotional pain management', and the wildly fluctuating hormones of pregnancy left me gripping onto Mal for emotional stability. It was a task he was ill-prepared for. It was a wild ride for both of us.

Pregnancy for me was really tough because I didn't have a great body image to begin with. Once that baby bump started to pop, I didn't feel in control of my body anymore. I hadn't realised how much of my self-esteem was tied to me looking a certain way. I remember one day in a carpark deciding I would slip between two cars, only to accidentally flip one of the mirrors with my tummy. I had no idea of the proportions of my belly, and it didn't feel like it belonged to me. I think that the moment I fell pregnant was the moment I began feeling my life was out of my control.

While some people talk about a joyful appreciation of the changes they are going through, I struggled to maintain a semblance of normality, as normality slipped through my fingers. During pregnancy, it's not just about you, it's also about the life growing inside you. Becoming a parent meant that I had to meet other people's needs, regardless of whether my needs were met or not. Having kids, starting with pregnancy, was like ripping off a band aid that was covering the selfish part of my soul that I didn't want anyone to see.

Coupled with that, I began to understand the gravity of the situation for Mal and myself. He had expectations for his baby and wanted the absolute best for us both. And that didn't seem to include all the rice crackers I had a craving for in the first twelve weeks. I was unprepared for the concept that my behaviour might impact his child (which was equally our child) and I didn't have the maturity to respond to that idea appropriately.

As I started to get a handle on the expectations of others which I hadn't considered, I met Mal's parents. They had flown from Sydney to Broome to meet me and to spend some time with Mal, and to holiday in Broome. Our baby would be their first grandchild. I was anxious to meet Mal's parents and was quite apprehensive. Would they judge me? Would they demand that we get married? What did they think of me?

All my fears faded when I met Marie and John. They were not judgemental. They were only supportive. I felt loved and accepted, even though I didn't really love and accept myself. I enjoyed their company, and I felt safe in their presence. I also noticed that they were different, in a good way, and very different from my parents. There was a loving kindness to Marie that I had never encountered. And there was a gentleness to John that I am sure is the vital ingredient of a 'gentleman' – something that seemed to have evaporated off the face of the earth, at least in my experience. My parents spent so much time 'ribbing' each other that you couldn't tell whether they were joking or throwing darts and barbs at each other. Marie and John just enjoyed each other and didn't say discouraging or disparaging things to each other, which was extremely novel to me. Perhaps there was a different way to do life?

Our son Liam was born in Broome, after a fairly straight forward pregnancy and a somewhat hectic delivery, into an extended family that would love and adore him. After twelve weeks of settling uncomfortably into parenthood, Mal and I moved to the east coast of Australia where we would eventually settle in Newcastle, New South Wales. We wanted to be closer to family; Broome felt a long way away from everyone. It seemed natural to Mal to move closer to home where his family could support us. And as I had absolutely no idea what I was doing, I agreed.

Leaving Broome and the red dirt and the big blue sky was hard. It was the first time I had made good friends and settled into a community. Mal drove the Hilux back to Sydney over the course of seven days, with Kirby along for the ride, while Liam and I flew home to spend some time with my parents in Wangaratta, and then on to Sydney to stay with Mal's parents until we could find somewhere to live in Newcastle.

Surrounded by the love of Mal's extended family, we moved to Newcastle. We left behind everything that had helped me cope with life. I left my job, the open spaces, the friends and the lifestyle of the tropics. It was time to start again, and I was terrified of what would come next.

CHAPTER 18

BAKING A CAKE WITHOUT A RECIPE

For me, being a mother was like trying to bake a cake without a recipe. I had a vague idea of the vital ingredients required, but absolutely no idea how to put it all together. I read lots of books and gleaned lots of helpful information from Marie. She seemed to have an endless supply of tips and tricks for Liam and bucketfuls of love to give. I still felt like the bucket that should contain and hold my love had a leak, and I didn't quite know how to love Liam or Mal or my new extended family. I was like a deer in the headlights, wondering which way to run, but realising that this time, running wasn't an option.

There are lots of experts on parenthood. As a new Mum, you tend to run into them when you are struggling in the supermarket or juggling a baby and other seemingly simple tasks. Complete strangers would walk up to me in the street and offer me sage advice. And if that wasn't somewhat overwhelming at times, there was another sort of parenting expert who would share a passing comment instead of a tip. They would say things like, 'these are the best days of your life', or something similar. I didn't seem to be experiencing 'normal' emotions as a new mother. Again, I felt like I was doing something wrong. I had missed something vital, and my emotions had been left behind in the delivery ward. Most days I just felt tired and numb.

I also felt like I was failing miserably at motherhood because my son would spend a large percentage of the day uncomfortable or crying. Liam suffered from colic or reflux, and the simple task of digestion was unpleasant and uncomfortable for him. I had never truly appreciated the benefits of a good burp before I became a Mum. And, might I add, a good burp is one where only gas comes up. I was also perplexed at the vast number of ways a parent could burp their baby, and although effortless and effective for others, none of them seemed to be reliably effective for me.

Poor Liam also spent a surprising amount of time vomiting or regurgitating. He would vomit when I picked him up and when I put him down. He would vomit every time I tried to buckle him into a car seat or a stroller and nearly every time we lifted him out of such a device. My life was full of milky vomit and bunny rugs, towels, wipes and dirty laundry, not to mention sleepless nights. Even when I thought I was having a good day managing the supermarket without a screaming baby, I would get the tap on the shoulder and a complete 'stranger - expert' would inform me that I had vomit all down my back. Without really meaning to, I added a new narrative to the thoughts swirling in my head - 'I'm not a good mother' - because I wasn't overcome with love for my gorgeous baby boy.

I didn't know what to do ... and because I didn't like it when I didn't know what to do, I went back to doing something I did know how to do - I found a new veterinary job in Newcastle. Going back to work allowed me to clutch at some normality in a very busy and a very challenging season. For the next few years I didn't have the luxury, or indulgence of self-reflection or self-awareness. I got stuck in survival mode and the years started to grind by.

My endless search for satisfaction continued. I had a truly good human to do life with. Mal was endlessly patient and supportive of me. I had an engaging and curious young son who was discovering life with joy and excitement. But, it seemed that meeting my life partner and becoming a Mum weren't going to satisfy the dull ache inside for validation, acceptance and fulfilment. I re-entered the treadmill of trying to find 'that thing' that would make my life complete.

At around the same time, my Dad was diagnosed with bowel cancer. He had stoically ignored his symptoms right up to the point that his bowel obstructed. After an emergency surgery to relieve the obstruction, Dad was scheduled to have the mass removed. What ensued was a painful journey for Dad and the whole family as he battled cancer. Sadly, he started fighting long after the 'horse had bolted' and he didn't really ever stand a chance. Years of drinking had also destroyed his liver, so he couldn't produce enough protein to heal from his surgical wounds. His agonising illness ended barely eight months later.

At the time my Dad died, I hadn't processed my childhood experiences. Most of the pain of my childhood abuse had been buried in a dark recess of my soul, and it didn't surface when my Dad was sick. My Dad had become an orphan at sixteen and was abandoned by his extended family and grew up on his wits and intelligence alone. He didn't know how to be a father because he hadn't been fathered. Drinking had been a coping mechanism for the best part of his life. He did the best he could with what he knew and the hand he had been dealt.

As the doctors took care of his symptoms at the end of his struggle, he slipped into a medical coma. I wasn't sure if anything

I said would be heard, but I told him, 'thanks for being the best Dad in the world'.

As I finished my sentence, I held my Dad's hand, and he took his last breath.

Being with Dad as he died was a very personal and special moment that would be a blessing in years to come. Grief is complicated, and my emotions as my Dad died were chaotic and confused. I became desperate to find a meaning to this crazy life we were living. And wherever I looked, I found dead ends. I was clueless as to what it was all about.

In the months following Dad's death, Mal and I bought a house in a lovely seaside suburb in Newcastle and we started to make Newcastle our home. Mal knew I was unsettled, and didn't know how to help, but remembering that scuba diving was where I had experienced a sense of peace and calm previously, Mal and I planned an adventure to Palau. We went scuba diving with Manta Rays, sharks and amazing reef and tropical fish, while Liam established a beautiful bond with his doting grandparents.

Because travel had scratched an itch in my soul previously, we also travelled overseas as a young family to explore Italy. We visited close friends who were spending time with relatives for a few months in a regional Italian community and immersed ourselves in a new culture with our very energetic two-year-old. It was great. Afterwards, however, we decided to keep our travel domestic until Liam was older.

Following our trip to Italy, Mal embarked on an ambitious plan to renovate and expand our house, while we were still living in it. And soon after our Italian holiday, my midriff began to expand again as we awaited the birth of our second child. Midway through the renovation, when there was no exterior cladding on the walls, a tarp was covering the roof, the hot water system was being swapped over, and the power was out because the switchboard was being replaced ... I went into labour.

We welcomed Olivia into our family; she barely noticed the chaos of our living arrangements. I was blessed the second time around with a little baby girl who only cried when she was starving, and she didn't vomit ... not once. She was full of joy and energy (until she wasn't) and she slept beautifully to recharge her batteries. Perhaps I was a good mother after all!

When Liam started school and Olivia was barely eighteen months old, I studied for and completed my membership with the Australian College of Veterinary Scientists in Small Animal surgery. I was still searching for recognition and validation, this time in my career. I had hoped that gaining this particular qualification would lead to new and better job opportunities and increase both my professional recognition and personal fulfilment. It took a year of studying during the evening hours after the kids had settled in bed. The time sacrifice was significant, and Mal covered all the gaps in my parenting duties as I studied. I was overjoyed and relieved to pass those exams. But while the qualification added some letters behind my name, it didn't fill any of the gaps in my soul.

Moving to Newcastle also placed us back in proximity to Mal's childhood friends and I started to get to know the people Mal had grown up with. One of the things that quickly became a regular feature in our lives was a trip to Mal's friends, Trix and Jill, who lived on a farm near Ellenborough. Every Easter, we would camp on their farm with a bunch of other families with kids. It became a vital time to relax and recharge. They say it takes a village to raise a child. Making connections during those Easter farm visits made me feel that I had a village to support me, and I began to hope that I had an outside chance of raising our children past infancy.

It was around the campfire at Easter that we would talk about kids, growth spurts, behavioural phases, feeding, day care, kindergarten and education, development and every other thing that I needed to know about. In Jill and Trix there was a peace that reminded me of Marie and John. There was less of a focus on what you do, or what you or your children had achieved, and more of a delight in who you were. There was joy, love and peace in abundance. I knew I didn't have that, and I wanted it. There was another way of doing life and I was curious to know what that was.

When Sunday rolled around and Jill and Trix invited me to church, I politely declined. And they were okay with that. I was also okay that Mal went with them. It was Easter after all. Mal had shared with me about his childhood, his church upbringing and his Mum and Dad's strong faith. I was surrounded by his friends, and they were all good people, but I hadn't really met Christians before and didn't associate their love, peace and joy with their faith.

Outside of Easter, Mal and I would often go and spend the weekend with Marie and John in Sydney. When Marie and John went to church, they would take Liam, and then also Olivia when she came along, and Mal and I would have time to read the paper and have a quiet coffee in a nearby cafe. I liked that Marie and John took the kids to church. They carved out these delicious moments of time for us to be together, in an otherwise very busy life.

So, life rolled on and the kids grew. Life became even busier. I was trying to juggle work, kids, daycare and school and my relationship with Mal. My inner narrative hadn't changed, and I didn't know how I would keep going. I just didn't feel that I had what it took. I was at a particularly low ebb approaching my fortieth birthday. Forty seemed old, but I felt like I was still twenty in my head. My body, however, felt like it was forty and that was depressing. In the days leading up to my birthday, I had been in hospital with dangerously low blood pressure and a severe viral infection. I made it out of hospital just in time to jump on a plane for a surprise holiday that Mal had arranged to celebrate my big day.

We flew to Hamilton Island and had a beautiful few days enjoying the island together with Marie and John. One afternoon, while Marie and John were minding Liam and Olivia, Mal and I went for a walk. We walked out along the jetty, and I wondered out loud if one day we could hire a yacht. I was worried about the kids and while they had both had plenty of swimming lessons, living on a yacht would present a constant risk. Mal gave me a cheeky smile and said, 'not just yet'.

The next day, Marie and John flew home, and we caught a ferry back to the mainland, followed by a taxi to Queensland Yacht Charters. I expected that we would be enjoying Airlie Beach for a few days before flying home. I did not expect to see Jill and Trix and their three kids loading a week's worth of groceries onto a catamaran. Mal was bubbling with excitement. 'Happy Birthday!' It was the most thoughtful, beautiful gift I could imagine. A week with friends, sailing the Whitsundays.

Jill and Trix had three amazing kids, all just that little bit older than Liam and Olivia. We quickly established some rules around lifejackets and Jill's oldest daughter, Maddie, graciously included Liam and Olivia in all of the kid's games and made sure that Olivia had her lifejacket on when they were walking around the boat or up the front. The extra sets of eyes certainly calmed my nerves and so we set off for a week of sailing around the Whitsundays.

Mal and I were both still recovering from a lingering virus and the weather was a little grey and rainy to begin with, but as the week progressed, the sun came out and my mood started to lift too. Being on the water has always calmed my soul. There is something therapeutic for me about swimming in the ocean. Immersing myself in deep blue water restores me in a way that is hard to explain. We swam, we snorkelled, and we sailed for seven beautiful days.

When Mal returned to Newcastle, he decided it was time to find a church. Again, I was completely fine with that. I immediately anticipated regular time to myself on a Sunday morning, which was an extremely rare commodity in that season. I could envision a relaxing coffee and undisturbed reading time and had absolutely no objections to Mal's new desire for our family.

It took me by surprise though, one morning, when Liam asked if I would come with the family to church. I was taken aback by Liam's newly expressed faith and his earnest desire that I would learn about Jesus too. I was immediately very anxious about church. Would they know I wasn't a Christian? Can non-believers go to church? Would they judge me? We weren't even married. How would that go??

Mal sensed my rising anxiety. 'It's okay, we can sit up the back. If you want, you can close your eyes and have a rest. I can show you what to do.'

I wondered if that's what church was all about, but I agreed. I had never been to church before. My Mum had had some negative experiences with church and claimed that Christians were judgemental. Having met Mal's friends and his Mum and Dad I knew that wasn't always the case, but walking into that church was possibly the hardest thing I have ever done.

CHAPTER 19

BUILDING ON A ROCK

Church wasn't what I expected it to be. It was a small local church with a bunch of families with kids of similar ages to ours. People were very nice to me, and I was a little excited to find out that they had good coffee. I could still enjoy my Sunday coffee after all!

Growing up I had played the piano and music was a big part of my childhood, but I was never any good at singing. In church it seemed to me that there was a lot of singing. I stood there on that first day, quite embarrassed, mouthing the words to the songs on the overhead projection in front of me, songs that I didn't know. I looked around the room. People were singing from their souls, proclaiming their love for Jesus and they seemed to be genuinely happy. I had seen this phenomenon in Jill one Easter. As she prepared lunch for nearly twenty-five people, she was singing the songs she had sung earlier in the day at church and seemed totally at peace in the process. It was an enigma that I didn't grasp at all.

After the announcements, the kids went off to Sunday school and I was left to focus on the sermon. It was a bit like a lecture at university, and I had mastered the art of looking interested for hours of lectures through vet school, so I didn't think this would be a problem. I thought it would be rude to close my eyes like Mal had suggested.

I remember that sermon as if it were yesterday. The pastor was talking about a wise man who built his house on a rock. When the wind and waves came, the house stood firm. And then there was the foolish man who built his house on the sand. His house could not withstand the storm. I was intrigued. In that moment I knew that I had built my life on the sand, and I was sinking. But how did I get on the rock, and who would help me shift my house? Could I keep everything in my house and translocate, or did I have to build again from scratch?

I had questions. Lots of questions. And I was desperate to know the answers. I was like a labrador at lunch time, hungry for any scrap that someone would throw me. I started reading the Bible. I became frustrated with the Bible. I wanted to flick to the back of the Bible like it was a maths textbook and find the solutions. Who had the answers? Was there a part B? Sometimes the Bible offended me, and I wanted to throw it across the room.

Within a few short months, I had signed up to a Bible study to learn more. Our church ran one on a Tuesday. On alternating weeks, it would be either the Mums' meeting or the Dads' meeting - so that there was always someone home with the kids. Mal and I both signed up and I had absolutely no idea what I was getting myself into.

I was just as nervous starting Bible study as I was when I walked into church. I knew nothing about the Bible, and I was nervous walking into a room full of people I didn't really know. People would quote things and reference things from the Bible in their regular conversation, and I had no idea what they were talking about. I was embarrassed by my complete lack of knowledge and understanding. It was a very uncomfortable feeling for me. The pastor's wife Judy ran the study, though, and I think she was the kindest and most patient person I had ever met at that time, and I was warmly welcomed.

But the other ladies were also lovely. There was cake and a cuppa and time to sit down and chat with a group of people who had that same love and peace which I so badly wanted in my life. I hadn't sat down and chatted with a group of friends regularly since I had left university. It was just as I imagined book club to be like, only there was tea instead of wine and we looked at the same book every week. I was welcomed and accepted, and I was encouraged to ask all of my questions. That gorgeous group of women became my dear friends in a very short space of time.

Not all of my questions had easy answers. Sometimes my questions made the group shift uncomfortably in their seats. Sometimes I would just get 'that's a really good question and you have a good point there'. And lots of the material in the study made me uncomfortable too. I found it really hard to accept that Jesus loved me. How did He even know me? Did He know what I had been up to for the last forty years? It took me months to wrap my head around that concept, and many others.

As someone who had grown up fascinated with science, and who had a career in veterinary science, I wanted to know if God and science could co-exist. I wanted to know about creation and understand if there was space for evolution in that theory. Was creation evolving? Did it really say seven days? Where did the dinosaurs fit in?

At the end of every study session and after discussion we would pray. I sat there for weeks, wondering what prayer was all about. I was too shy to put any requests forward and way too shy to say anything. But I sat amongst them, and marvelled at my friends' faith that God would step into their everyday lives to help them if He was asked. I wanted to get to know who God was, before I asked Him for anything. I also wanted to clean up my act before I talked to God. I was certain that He wouldn't talk to someone like me anyway.

So, I read a lot of books about God and about the Bible. I was so hungry for information I would have my friends give me two or three books at a time. Everyone seemed to have a suggestion for what might be helpful. And I read voraciously. Marie and John were very invested in feeding me books and I peppered Mal with an endless array of questions. Sometimes we had great discussions and sometimes we didn't.

Nearly one year into our attendance at church, Mal and I and the kids planned to go on half-a-lap trip around Australia. It was the year before Olivia went to school and it was a great opportunity for us to spend quality time together, doing what we loved to do - explore this great country of ours with our kids. I was excited to be getting back into the bush, back to the red dirt and blue sky that I loved so much. The peace and the space would be a welcome change from the hustle of our lives in Newcastle.

Our church kindly gave us a devotional to do while we were away. It was called the *Purpose Driven Life*, by Rick Warren. My Bible study ladies also bought me a gift - my very own Bible. And with those two resources in hand, we packed the Landcruiser and the van to the gunnels, squashed the kids into the back seat with a bucket full of toys and books, and headed off.

It was the morning of day two into our trip when we opened up our devotional. I liked the idea of a 'purpose driven life'. I really wanted someone to tell me what my purpose was. Maybe this book would hold some valuable keys. I was shocked when I read the first line of this book.

'It's not about you.'

It felt like the book was speaking directly to me and I wanted to throw that book out of the window. What on EARTH do you mean?

My Dad had always told me to be selfish in pursuit of my goals. He had been forced to be selfish in pursuit of his goals to survive. I had always been determined to set my goals and meet them, and his advice had served me well so far. I had no framework for this kind of thinking. Deep in my heart I also knew I was quite selfish. And as I read that line a thousand thoughts flooded my consciousness, supporting my selfishness. My Dad had always encouraged me to be independent and self-sufficient, and to solve problems and meet my own needs. I thought I was pretty good at meeting my own needs. I had never before contemplated the possibility that my life was not about me.

It was challenging for me to process another point of view. I would often read the devotional in printed form in the book, while the family listened to the audio version on CD in the car. Sometimes there would be plenty of discussion, sometimes I would feel angry or threatened or alone in my own thoughts. It brought up loads more questions and sometimes I had very difficult conversations with Mal. At times it was nearly a relief to switch over to another audiobook such as Robinson Crusoe, or the battle-weary selection of The Wiggles we had lined up for the kids, because I found the devotional so confronting.

So, our family holiday of a lifetime became an interesting journey of exploring new territory, both physically and internally. As we travelled deep into the outback, I felt like I had the time and space to question what I believed. I had space to consider if Dad had got it right, and to imagine myself trying on a different style of thinking - to see if it would fit. It also became quite clear to me, that if I was to try on a new way of thinking, I would have to discard a lot of the belief system that was ingrained in my heart and soul. I wasn't quite sure how that process would actually happen, and what it would take for me to make the change.

Towards the second half of our travels, we were on our way back from visiting Uluru, the iconic red rock in the middle of Australia. We had eyed the diesel prices in Yulara, the township servicing the tourist industry at Uluru, before leaving. We both considered that their prices were unfair and outrageous, and we decided that we would drive to a little roadhouse situated around halfway back to the Stuart Highway.

It was with some alarm, however that we discovered that the little roadhouse at halfway was closed that day, awaiting a fuel delivery. Mal and I looked at each other. We were about to enter new territory of a different kind. Mal knew our Landcruiser inside out. He knew how far it would go on a full tank loaded, unloaded and towing a van. Of course, we were fully loaded and towing a caravan, and he just looked at me and said,

'I don't think we can make it back to the highway.'

It was too far to go back; we had to keep going. Mal slowed down to a very moderate pace, and we turned off the air conditioner and wound down the windows instead, trying to conserve as much fuel as possible.

We were about 10 km short of the roadhouse on the Stuart highway when we sputtered to a stop, out of fuel. It was in that moment that I thought I would try talking to God. It wasn't a prayer as such, more of a quick question to see if He cared about our situation, in that moment, in the middle of nowhere, with our young family. 'God, if you're real, if you're listening...we need your help,' I asked internally. It was more of a thought than a spoken prayer.

Mal had pulled off to the side of the road and had popped the bonnet on the Landcruiser to signal that we needed help. I wasn't sure how long we would be waiting. It felt dangerous beside the road with two young kids, even though there wasn't a lot of traffic. It was hot, we were isolated. We could see no other signs of life, all the way to the horizon in every direction. We felt very alone...for roughly 90 seconds.

That was when we saw another ute approaching. It was a station vehicle, and I felt relief wash over my body. Even if they couldn't help us, they may have a radio, or a way of getting help to us. The station vehicle pulled up across the road.

'What's up', the station guy asked as he rolled down his window and adjusted the wide-brimmed hat on his head.

'We've run out of diesel,' Mal said.

'Which side is your tank?' The guy asked.

'Left side,' Mal said.

Straight away, the station guy drove across the road and pulled up beside our car. On the back of the ute was a tank of diesel with a hose and pump ... just like a mobile service station. As he started to fill the tank, he mentioned that he owned the service station up the road. He also ran the cattle station surrounding the roadhouse. He was a lovely guy, very matter of fact and refused to take any money for the fuel. And in no more than five minutes we were on our way.

As we started our car, Mal and I looked at each other. It was a surreal moment. I told Mal that I had prayed to God and Mal told me he had too. God had answered us in an amazing way. Yes, God was real. Yes, God cared about us, in that moment, in the middle of nowhere. My mind was spinning. I could no longer deny God. And God was good. Unbelievably good to us, in our moment of need. I was just a little bit freaked out that God had answered my 'thought' prayer in such a practical, instantaneous way.

I had been stranded in the outback before, with flat tyres or car problems in my working days, driving between clinics or station calls. I had often waited more than an hour for another vehicle to pass by in some of the more remote locations I had worked. I had often driven hours on lonely roads without seeing another vehicle … and I had never prayed to God to help me before.

I had never imagined a God who could hear my thoughts and deliver on my request within seconds. How did God know me? How did God know my thoughts? I hadn't even made a commitment to God when he answered my prayer that day. So, for the next few days I sat in that uncomfortable space of knowing God exists but being afraid to make a commitment to Him. I still had so much to figure out, so much to learn and so much to process. And somewhere in the bush, out behind the back of beyond, I decided that I would give God a go. I had tried everything I knew to do and had wound up tired, exhausted and frustrated, and yet I had just experienced His goodness. A goodness that was worth the leap of faith. Goodness that I was nervous to trust, but I would trust with my very broken 'truster' and see what happened next. I said another internal prayer to God, and we continued on our way.

I didn't announce my decision to anyone for a few days, and I can't recall Mal making a big deal of it. But when I told my pastor at our local church a month or two later, he seemed a little concerned for me. He hadn't picked up on any change and he was wondering if I had received the gift of the Holy Spirit. So, our pastor did something he hadn't done before in our church. He asked everyone to close their eyes and bow their heads, and he asked if anyone wanted to receive Jesus as their Lord and Saviour at the end of our service.

I knew my pastor was speaking to me, and I was a little irritated. I didn't need to put my hand up, I had already made my decision. But in that moment, something crazy happened with my heart. It started rattling in my chest in a way that I had never experienced before. My heart was thumping physically in my chest and resounding in my ears. I heard a little whisper in my soul tell me to put my hand up. So, I did.

Making a commitment to Jesus seemed a much bigger deal to everyone around me than it did to me. I was a little confused as to why people wanted to celebrate my decision as I was nervously trying to step in a new direction. It only made sense later, when I learnt that my church friends, Mal's friends and Mal's Mum and Dad had been faithfully praying for us while we were away. There were a lot of people that were emotionally and spiritually invested in my progress. At the same time, I started to appreciate that there was a power in prayer that I didn't understand. I had felt it in the desert, and I saw it on my friends' faces at church. There is a joy associated with asking the Creator of the universe to help you and subsequently seeing God step into the physical realm in practical, loving and helpful ways.

And I wanted to know more.

CHAPTER 20

GOLD DUST

I was given lots of good advice when I became a follower of Jesus. My Bible study friends had lots of resources, books, DVDs and pastors' podcasts for me to listen to. But the one that made the biggest impact came  from a friend called Stacey. She gave me a book called *Dreaming with God* by Bill Johnson, and she then invited me along to a meeting in a little church in Pelican. There was a team visiting from Bethel Church in Redding, California, which was actually the church that Bill Johnson pastored. As we were walking in, she was giving me a brief about what I might expect.

Stacey smiled as she told me that our little Baptist church in Jewells was quite conservative. She told me that all sorts of things might happen, and not to be worried or scared. She reminded me that God is good and that it will be fun. She told me a little bit about God the Father, Jesus the son and the Holy Spirit. I was pretty familiar with God the creator of the Universe, and while I was still not sure how He did it, I was ready to accept that the work of His hands was truly magnificent. I was familiar with Jesus. Our church taught a lot on Jesus, and I had been reading my Bible on our half-a-lap holiday, so I was familiar with the stories and the Gospel. But I was not familiar with the Holy Spirit. That was about to change.

The worship and singing started and it was immediately different to our little church in Jewells. People in this church were dancing. Some people were waving flags. The songs were long and seemed to have endless chorus repeats. I was standing with Stacey and her husband Tim, and trying to figure everything out, but I decided that it was a bit overwhelming, especially visually... so I closed my eyes. And I relaxed and started to let my mind wander as I focused on the words of the worship songs. Random images started to infiltrate my consciousness as I swayed to the music. This felt good.

As the worship finished the team from Bethel were introduced and they started talking about the goodness of God. They started calling out people to stand up for healing prayer. I had no idea what was going on, but Stacey explained everything as it was happening. As people were prayed for some fell over. I was quite shocked. I was genuinely concerned that instead of healing, they might hurt themselves. Stacey told me that it was the power of the Holy Spirit. In that moment I exchanged another thought prayer with God and told Him as politely as I could, that I would very much like to NOT fall over under the power of the Spirit. Please God, don't let that happen to me.

But then some people began to testify that they had been healed of chronic, painful conditions. How could that be, I wondered? Stacey explained that healing is the character and nature of God. I had never heard of such a thing, I did remember that Jesus healed a lot of people in the Bible. But I had no reference for a Jesus who had existed on planet earth over two thousand years ago, healing people in the here and now in a church that was a converted bowling club in Pelican, NSW.

Then another team member from Bethel told a testimony of a lady who had been healed on the Central Coast during the week. The team had been praying for her, and she had been covered in gold dust. She had been completely healed. Then the girl giving the testimony got excited, and she said, 'Look at your hands, the gold dust is here too. God wants to heal you too.'

I looked at my hands and couldn't believe what I was seeing. My hands, fingers and half of my forearms were covered in gold dust. My skin was glittering. Tim and Stacey looked at their hands. Tim had gold dust on the tips of his fingers. Stacey had no gold dust at all. I started looking around to see if there was a trick. Was there gold dust on the chairs, or had I brushed up against something? I had absolutely no explanation for what was going on and my brain started to hurt.

Stacey put her hand on my shoulder and prayed for me in that moment, and she prayed for Tim too. I had no idea what it meant, but it was exciting. I learnt that night that God has gold too. I took my gold home and showed Mal. He was perplexed. In all of his life as a Christian, he hadn't ever experienced gold dust in a church meeting. I started to believe in a God with endless possibilities.

REMEMBERING THE PAIN

I have always had a very busy brain. It works way too hard. At that time in my life, there were too many words, too many thoughts and too many internal narratives. In amongst that chaos, I discovered God was trying to speak to me. Because He couldn't get a word in edgeways during the day, I started having vivid dreams. Now, I have always been a dreamer, and I have always remembered my dreams. But for the first time in my life, I had a sense that some of these dreams were about God trying to show me things.

One such dream happened while I was awake, sort of like a daydream - but maybe like a technicolour vivid flashback.

I was in my childhood bedroom. My Dad was 'kissing' me goodnight. Like he always did. Like he had done every night, since before I could remember.

My Mum walks past the door and looks in. She stands in the doorway, a look of horror on her face. She yells at my Dad and my Dad scuttles out of the room. She points an angry finger in my direction and her words pierced my heart.

I felt God whispering to me... 'this is where we start'.

COLOUR

The next pivotal moment in my walk with Jesus was at a ladies' conference in Sydney run by Hillsong Church called 'Colour'. It was reassuring to be there with Stacey and all of the ladies from our Bible study. I had no idea what to expect and was awestruck from the moment that it started. There were over ten thousand women, worshipping God in beautiful unity and harmony. The atmosphere in that room was extraordinary.

There were a number of different speakers, but one completely rocked my world. Her name was Lisa Bevere. She spoke very openly and vulnerably about her family. She had had a difficult relationship with her father, and he had been an alcoholic. There are no benign alcoholics. She told a courageous story of her childhood pain, her journey of forgiveness and the miraculous salvation of her Dad before he passed away.

I had never heard a sermon like this before. It was raw and honest and life changing for me. In that moment, I no longer felt alone and isolated. There was someone else in the world with a hard family story and they were prepared to talk about it, rather than hide in the dark, covered in shame. Lisa's sermon was about 'Girls with Swords'. Not a sword of vengeance or revenge, but a sword of the Word of God. She talked about laying down her anger and her pain and picking up the Word of God to fight her battles. She offered me a choice. A way to deal with my pain and shame.

As the band returned to start singing, I felt like something opened up within me. Years of pent-up tears started to flow. Violent sobs started to contort my body, and I had absolutely no control over what was happening. I didn't usually cry. I hadn't cried for years. And I had never cried in public before, not since I was three. My friends rallied for tissues and Stacey stood by me with a hand on my back, praying for me in the moment.

The words of the song penetrated my soul. It felt like the song was for me. In a stadium of ten thousand women, the band was singing a song for me. They were the words I needed in that moment, when only tears would flow.

Sinking Deep
(Hillsong Young and Free)
Standing here, in your presence
In a grace, so relentless
I am won
By perfect love
Wrapped within the arms of heaven,
In a peace that lasts forever
Sinking deep
In mercy's sea.
I'm wide awake,
Drawing close, stirred by grace
And all my heart is yours,
All fear removed
I breathe you in, I lean into your love.

I had an experience of God's love in that moment, and it was overwhelming. It was powerful and healing and just a little bit scary at the same time. I have never felt a love like that before. A love that held me and said, 'you're going to be okay. I know how you're hurting...and I can help you. Let's walk this path together.' I felt protected and safe and understood. It was like God's heart knew everything that had ever happened to me and still loved me anyway. I didn't have to earn this love; it just washed over me.

When it was time to leave, I couldn't move. I didn't want to move. I wanted to stand there worshipping my God. There were dinner plans though, and a massive seething crowd to make our way through, to reach our restaurant in Darling Harbour. Stacey leaned into my ear and said, 'I have just seen your heart transformed from a heart of stone to a heart of flesh'... and she quoted me this Bible verse:

I will give you a new heart and put a new spirit in you; I will remove from you your heart of stone and give you a heart of flesh. And I will put my Spirit in you and move you to follow my decrees and be careful to keep my laws. (Ezekiel 36: 26-27)

I was shaking like a leaf. I was still crying, and I couldn't stop. And my legs didn't work. Stacey and Louise helped me along, through the crowd and onto the forecourt to walk to our restaurant. People were looking at me as if I was strange. I felt strange. I felt as if a bomb had just gone off in my heart and all of my emotions were exposed and leaking. I didn't even feel as if I was in my body. I didn't really want to talk at dinner, and I didn't really want to eat dinner. I just wanted to know what God was up to.

The God that sprinkled me with gold dust was now doing divine heart surgery and there were no anaesthetists or operating rooms. It seemed as if it should have been a very private operation, but here I was in a crowd. I had set some wheels in motion and in that moment of giving my heart to God, I felt that my life wasn't my own anymore. I certainly didn't feel as if I was in charge, that's for sure.

HEART RESTORATION

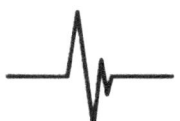

Returning from 'Colour' was tricky. I had been in a divine atmosphere with my friends for three days and I didn't want to leave. I had experienced the love of God for the first time, and it was like a drug I couldn't get enough of. I wanted more. I had also experienced the presence of God and the Holy Spirit. I wanted more of that too. And I didn't feel the Holy Spirit in our church, and that bothered me deeply. So, I started hunting out that feeling in a range of different meetings and gatherings.

Stacey invited me to another meeting run by a pastor named Steven Clarke. I trusted Stacey, so I was keen to go. Steve was an interesting character. He certainly didn't look like a pastor. He looked more like someone who was a member of bikie gang, without the leather and the patches. Stacey knew Steve well and introduced me to him. Steve looked me over as we came into the meeting.

'How's your family?' he asked me, completely out of the blue.

I didn't know how to answer that question. My immediate family or my family of origin? At times both were pretty chaotic. It felt like he was reading my mail. I was still fumbling with an answer when he said, 'you're in the right place, take a seat.'

Stacey started to explain that Steve had a strong prophetic gift. He had visions and prophetic words for people all the time. Steve and his wife Tanya also had a powerful healing ministry. I knew I needed healing, even though I didn't know what that would entail. I felt that God had given me a starting point - the childhood trauma and abuse I experienced growing up in my family, but I felt the biggest problem at that time was my relationship with Mal, and figuring out how to be a parent.

The sessions were conducted over the course of the day, and they were just what I needed. I had moment after moment of knowing that what Steve and Tanya were talking about was the truth because it resonated deep inside of me. At the end of the day, Steve offered to speak some prophetic words over people. Stacey encouraged me to go up, and sensing my reluctance, we went up together. I had no idea what that would be like either. I didn't record that word, but I do remember that Steve looked me in the eye and said that I had been wounded by my mother. He declared that God wanted to heal me of those wounds. I didn't really 'hear' the rest of the words he spoke, because I spent the rest of the time wondering how on earth he knew that I had a mother wound, and what that meant. Stacey told me that Steve could 'hear' things from God or 'see' things from God and the prophetic word was a way for us to connect to God, especially when we weren't seeing or hearing things ourselves.

At the end of the meeting, I picked up a brochure for a weeklong healing retreat called 'Restore'. It was held in the Blue Mountains, at Steve's church. And so it was that several months later, I was in the Blue Mountains embarking on a healing retreat with absolutely no idea what the sessions would be about. (I didn't even know if I should pack my swimmers for the soaking prayer!) I just knew I needed to go.

On the morning of day one I decided I would sneak a quick trip to the bathroom before everything got started. I was just exiting a cubicle, when I found another lady in the bathroom at the sink, a little fixated on something. I asked if she was OK, and she said that she was trying to figure out if the insect in the sink was a bee or a wasp.

It was indeed a wasp. I suggested that we should open the window to let it out.

It was an old building, which in its former life had been a golf club. The sash windows were swollen and difficult to move. I grabbed the latch, and the lady helped me to push the window up. I am not sure what happened next or how, but the window came smashing down on both of my hands. The pain was instantly excruciating. I was able to drag my right hand out from the window, scraping all of my fingers in the process, and the lady helped me to lift up the window so I could release my left hand.

In that moment I knew something was seriously wrong with my fingers. The bruising on my middle and ring fingers came up rapidly and it felt like they were swelling before my eyes. I couldn't feel any sensation on the inside or outside of my ring finger on my left hand, and I was worried that I might have damaged those nerves. I couldn't believe it. I had broken a finger before, when Livi was a baby. I had shut the car door on my hand and had needed surgery to heal my pinkie finger on the right hand. I knew what it felt like to have a broken finger. Just my luck, I thought angrily, here I am at a healing retreat, and I will have to go to hospital, have X-rays and might need surgery.

The lady and I came out of the bathroom, and she was desperate to get me some help. I think she felt responsible for the window falling on my fingers. Moments later I was standing in front of Steve. He was an intimidating man. He was bald, he had a luxuriant grey goatee beard and a sizeable frame. He looked at me and asked, 'Why are you crying?'

The lady started filling him in on what had happened. She was beside herself. Steve quickly delegated two people to go with her into the front room and help her to calm down. Then he asked another lady to go and get me some ice from the kitchen.

He looked at me with what I interpreted to be annoyance, but maybe it was irritation.

'Be healed in Jesus' name,' Steve said, with one hand on my shoulder.

I guess it was a prayer, but I had never heard a prayer like that before.

'Now, go sit up the front and take these tissues with you,' he said rather dispassionately as the band began to play.

I went up the front as I was told with a tea towel of ice on my left hand, annoyed, frustrated and feeling very sorry for myself, with hot tears of embarrassment still streaming down my face. I didn't know whether to stay or go, and what the wait times would be like in the ER at the end of the day. My medical brain was in overdrive. With Steve's eyes on me though, I didn't have the courage to walk out and go to the hospital, so I started to worship.

I don't remember if it was in the first song, but it felt like just minutes later, that I felt a gentle brush down my right hand and instantly the pain was gone. It was like a physical touch. I opened my eyes, but there was no-one beside me. Inside my head I said, 'thank you God, at least I'll be able to take notes now', because I was a right-hander and note-taking was my established learning pattern after years of study.

But a little later into the worship something quite extraordinary started happening on my left hand. It became hot. Hot like I have never experienced before. Hot from the inside out. I opened my eyes again and realised that I still had ice strapped to my hand. My busy brain was still trying to figure things out. My hand was hot. I had ice strapped to my hand. This doesn't make sense. And then the pain disappeared from my left hand as well. I could move my fingers. I still had the odd lack of sensation along the inside and the outside of the finger, but it didn't hurt.

'Thank you, God!' I whispered out loud. 'What just happened?' I asked out loud to no-one in particular.

And all of a sudden, the words on the screen for the songs that we were singing started to become my personal experience.

You are a God of the impossible.

You are worthy of praise.

I have spent my life devoted to the understanding of healing. My favourite part of veterinary science was surgery because I enjoyed putting broken things back together again. Surgery and especially orthopaedic surgery was my passion. I knew all about how to handle tissues gently and align bones properly, to improve the body's chances of healing well. But it would take weeks, especially with bones. In that moment I understood a different kind of healing.

God can heal in an instant.

God doesn't need a theatre to do surgery.

God can take the pain away.

I wouldn't have believed it to be possible, unless it had happened to me.

The rest of the week I spent, on the one hand, recounting God's miracle in my finger and feeling full of joy, and on the other having hot tears streaming down my face as another area of my wounded soul was exposed, again and again. The sessions were powerful and helpful, and my pain was deep. It seemed like I just couldn't stop crying. Something had happened at 'Colour' and was happening again at 'Restore'. My heart was open and raw. I couldn't control my tears - there was a well of them that seemed endless. In that space, I felt safe, and I didn't care. I don't wear mascara anyway, so what was the big deal with a few tears, I told myself.

And I wasn't alone. Everyone was there to get better. Some people looked pretty normal on the outside to me. But no-one can see a wounded soul. Steve seemed to know what was going on and was able to call out the lies and the thinking that perpetuated the pain, and to release it and bring healing.

By the end of the week, my testimony to the group was simple. If God can heal my finger, he can heal my heart.

CHAPTER 22

A FIRM PLACE TO STAND

I would have liked it if healing my heart happened in an instant. The truth was, and still is, that I am a work in process and God is still on the job, and likely will be, until I die.

God *can* heal in a heartbeat. But sometimes, he wants us to partner with Him. After my experience at 'Colour', I was feeling quite pleased that my heart of stone was gone and I was learning to work with my heart of flesh. The problem with this heart, though, was that I couldn't stop crying. I felt like an emotional wreck, a lot of the time. The only place I didn't completely lose it  was generally my workplace. There was a grace I experienced that allowed me to continue to go to work, help people and their pets and maintain my contribution to the family income. On both ends of those six to eight hours, I would spend a lot of time crying in my car while I was driving. I would leave for work early so that I could mop myself up and dry my tears before work. Sometimes after work, I would go for a walk and continue to cry and yell angry questions at God. I was exhausted, most of the time, and that was before I even started running the kids around to sports and cooking dinner.

In the moment I had invited Jesus to be my saviour I had received the Holy Spirit. The Holy Spirit is a free gift for every believer when they make a commitment to Jesus. The Holy Spirit is also called a 'helper '- the third person of the Trinity who helps us to become more like Jesus. (That is, if you listen to Him.) When the Holy Spirit wants me to do something, my heart beats out of my chest. He simply can't be ignored. Sometimes it's a physical response that a pastor calls for at the end of a sermon. Sometimes it's an unction that He wants me to act on.

It helps me to think of the Holy Spirit residing in my heart. But it's not always an easy fit. The Holy Spirit doesn't want to reside in a heart with a bunch of 'stinking thinking'. It's up to us to remove the old heart beliefs, the beliefs that don't line up with the word of God. Sometimes it can feel like a prickly relationship going on inside the heart. On one hand there is the third person of the Godhead, urging you on to do what is right and then there is a prickly mess, a residue of your life before the Holy Spirit moved in.

I started to learn that while I had the Holy Spirit and I had become a new creation at that moment of conversion, I also had a whole bunch of inner beliefs that were not Godly. As a result of my traumatic experiences, I had developed a narrative over time. The narrative of: -

I'm not good enough
I don't know enough
etc. etc.

Every experience I had in life, would either confirm or deny these heart beliefs. If I failed at work, or a patient died, it would reinforce that belief of 'not good enough'. It was like I had a sad little echidna living in my heart, full of bitterness, resentment, anger, disillusionment, hopelessness, isolation, who was unlovable, unworthy, and felt rejected, abandoned, full of pain, despair and unforgiveness. The echidna and the Holy Spirit were uncomfortable companions in the same heart.

Making a commitment to Jesus hadn't been an easy decision for me, but I didn't realise that walking it out would be challenging too. Everyone at church seemed so happy, everyone was so kind and generous and thoughtful, and I didn't feel good enough. Could God really love me? I tried really hard to be happy and kind and generous and thoughtful like everybody else, because I wanted to be. But I wasn't like everyone else, and I was exhausted from trying.

At some point I discovered that God didn't love me because *I* was good - He loved me because *He* was good. And I didn't have to do anything, except believe. I could stop trying and simply believe, stop earning and working, and receive. But while it had taken me a long time to believe, it took me much, much longer to receive all the love God had been waiting to give me. I still didn't think I deserved it. And I felt chained to the past, to a life I couldn't let go of. No matter how awful the cargo was, I didn't know I could live without my toxic load, with all of the prickles in my heart.

I kept fighting to keep my hold on what used to be, when God was trying to show me something new.

I had moments of little-by-little accepting God's love into my heart, but most of the time I was fighting, resisting, rationalising, running, hiding, making excuses and disbelieving that the God of the universe could love me. I spent a long time wrestling with God's love.

There is a cute bookmark in Christian bookstores that talks about two footprints in the sand going along the beach. (That's God walking with us, never leaving us or forsaking us.) And then one set of footprints disappeared. And the person asks God - why did you leave me? And God replies, that's when I carried you. This was not my Christian experience. My Christian experience was best described by Kris Vallotton from Bethel Church: *there wasn't two sets of footprints in the sand with me; there was one set of footprints and one set of drag marks, as I resisted every step of the way.*

It was hard for me to accept God's love into my heart, because of the pain in my life, caused by those who told me that they loved me... and then betrayed, abused, rejected abandoned and traumatised me. They had all told me that they loved me. And there were conditions on that love - I would be loved back if I did what they wanted, behaved a certain way, met goals or lofty standards. I had 'worked' all my life to be loved. And then God just simply loved me, prickles and all. God turned love upside down for me. It felt good.

But I also became mad and sad and desperate when I understood God's love. Because that kind of love, the love that loves despite all of the prickles, the love that soothes the pain of a broken life and a broken world and says - 'I've got this... trust me... everything is going to be okay', the love that restores a broken heart and puts broken things together again ... well, it just didn't seem to be so common on planet earth, and *everyone needed it.*

Jesus has showed us what love is meant to look like, so I went on a journey to learn how to love like Jesus. I felt as if I walked into the valley of the shadow of death. And Mal went on a journey too... but quite a different one. For a long time, I felt miles away. Loving people, as Jesus loved people, felt impossible for me. I couldn't love like Jesus while I carried so much pain. I couldn't love like Jesus with all of those prickles in my heart. At times I felt like I couldn't love at all. And somewhere in the valley, I fell into a pit of my own striving. It was a pit of utter despair. I realised I need to know Jesus, in order to love like Jesus. So, I looked in my

Bible to get to know Jesus. And I started talking to Him in earnest. (Jesus!!! Help me!!!!!)

That was when words started jumping at me off the page of my Bible. It felt as if the Bible was speaking to me.

He lifted me out of the slimy pit, out of the mud and mire, He set my feet on a rock and gave me a firm place to stand. (Psalm 40: 2)

And that was also when I started to see pictures in my mind during worship at church and dreaming in glorious Technicolor. And God, in all of His goodness would direct me to Scripture to confirm to me what He was trying to say. God started infiltrating my head and my heart.

Learning to love again was a slow process for me. I had to figure out where the prickles had become lodged in my heart and to remove them one by one. Each time the Holy Spirit would touch one of my prickles, I would know that He was working on something. I had a choice. Would I partner with the Holy Spirit in that moment, or would I try and deny it, ignore it and run away? Obedience was not my immediate response, a lot of the time. But I learnt in my disobedience that the process would be longer, slower, more drawn out and more painful. If I responded to the pastor who called out different people to stand for prayer (for example, people feeling that it was hard to forgive) and I stood, then somewhere deep inside, the Holy Spirit would do His divine heart surgery. The transformation of my heart is a mystery to me. All I know is, that on some level, I had to agree to it. The Holy Spirit will only work with a signed consent form.

The process of transformation began with my humble admission that I needed help. This was a problem I couldn't fix on my own. From that point on it became uniquely personal to me and my walk with God. But it was absolutely transactional; I had to surrender my pain and my heartache. Sometimes I had to surrender my right to be hurt or offended. Sometimes I needed to action forgiveness for someone who was responsible for my pain.

Instead of numbing my pain I had to explore it, experience it and then hand it to Jesus. I had to keep listening to the Holy Spirit and I had to do what He said, or the process stalled. Obedience to the Holy Spirit kept my heart tender and the healing process alive.

Jesus came to bind up the broken-hearted, to proclaim freedom for the captives, to release from darkness the prisoners, to proclaim the year of the Lord's favour and the day of vengeance of our God. He came to comfort all who mourn, to provide for those who grieve, to bestow on them a crown of beauty instead of ashes, the oil of joy instead of mourning, and a garment of praise instead of a spirit of despair. (Isaiah 61:1-4)

He came so that I would be free, free indeed. (John 8: 36)

He came so that I may have an abundant life. (John 10: 10)

As I read through these verses in the Bible, I became determined to continue the process until I felt free and could point my finger at an abundant life. I didn't feel that I had either within my grasp at the time, but I knew I had plenty of mourning, grief and ashes and I was looking to exchange them for joy, beauty and praise.

CHAPTER 23

DEALING WITH ADDICTION

*Be alert and of sober mind. Your enemy the devil prowls around
like a roaring lion, looking for someone to devour.*
(1 Peter 5:8)

When I first started working in the outback, I was young and bold and excited for every challenge that came my way. For example, I had no hesitation in accepting an equine patient in a tiny outback town called Meekatharra, the next time I travelled south to do the branch clinic run. The pony had been suffering from recurrent uveitis for a long time: it had a very sore, very blind eye. The owners were wanting to have the eye removed; to reduce the pain and suffering of the pony and I willingly agreed to perform the surgery.

We arranged to meet at the racetrack. The Members Lawn at the racetrack was the only patch of grass in the whole town, apart from the football field. The rest of the landscape, as far as the eye could see, was red dust. We met in the morning to avoid the heat of the day. I had mentally planned my procedure and had everything prepared and ready to go when my patient arrived.

I gave the sedatives into a big vein in my patient's neck and waited for the sleepiness to fall over my pony. After ten minutes, I looked at the owner and the pony and decided to give some more. My patient wasn't ready to be induced, and I didn't want the pony to fall into a light level of anaesthesia, so I rechecked my dose rates and gave some more drugs. And I waited. Once the pony's head hung low, I decided to give the next drug, the induction agent. The induction went smoothly, the pony very gracefully lay down, and I had my owner cradling the pony's head as I prepared for surgery.

It was only when I started to make my first surgical incision, that things started to go badly. The pony started to blink. My pony shouldn't be blinking, I told myself. I decided to give some more anaesthetic agent to deepen the plane of anaesthesia. After pausing a moment for the drugs to take effect, I started again.

Eye surgery nearly always turns my stomach. I had eye surgery on both of my eyes as a four-year-old. I remember the pain behind my eyeballs as I woke up, and I am unlikely to forget it. Doing eye surgery on any patient has always been challenging for me. But I was also quietly confident with this procedure. I had assisted an eye removal while I was at university, and I had performed an eye removal on a cow while I was on a rural student placement. I continued to work as quickly as I could, because I knew that the drugs didn't seem to be working the way they should in this little pony.

While I was working on the eye, nearly ready to remove it, I saw another blink, the pony's ear twitched, the face went into spasm and then the pony started to struggle. All four legs started thrashing violently. The pony kicked my surgical instruments, and they went flying across the lawn. With a whinny of terror, the pony sat up then stood up, flinging the owner to the ground. As the pony staggered around the lawn, my equipment, drugs, needles and syringes were trampled and crushed or scattered across the grass in the commotion. The pony stood on my foot, and I fell, awkwardly twisting my ankle. The owner was desperately trying to avoid flying hooves to recover the lead rope and calm the pony down. I scrambled to my feet and the pain in my ankle was nearly unbearable. I feverishly worked to get my hands on the sedatives and induction agents to top up the anaesthetic and get the procedure finished.

The adrenaline was pumping hard through my veins and my hands started to shake uncontrollably. Think! Calm down! I tried to regain control over my nerves. The pony staggered like a drunken sailor around the lawn, rearing up on one occasion, and falling against the guardrail of the racetrack. I watched in horror as I anticipated my patient coming down from that height with broken legs. I injected more sedative into the muscle, and when the owner could grab the lead rope again, we injected more drugs into the vein. I repeated my doses and then the pony went back down.

With no semblance of sterility left, I tried to disinfect the instruments that I could recover and finished the procedure. I took some local anaesthetic and infiltrated it around my surgical incision, trying to numb the area as an extra precaution while the pony was under general anaesthetic. My owner was sitting on his pony's neck, trying to prevent it from getting up and staggering around the lawn again. With shaking hands, I tied my last suture.

The owner slowly lifted his weight from the pony's neck and stood up. I moved my instruments and kit away from the pony's head and within seconds, the pony was back up on his feet. With a heady mix of wounded pride, intense embarrassment and professional shame, and feeling the pain in my ankle throbbing, I hobbled to the car, to get ten days' worth of broad-spectrum antibiotics and some tetanus shots for the pony.

Stage two anaesthesia is the state between consciousness and unconsciousness. It is the place where we can perceive pain, even though we are not fully aware of what is going on, and we are not in control of our body. Sometimes patients don't process drugs the way we would like or anticipate. On that horror-filled morning on the Members Lawn in Meekatharra, my patient went through stage two anaesthesia, because my drugs, unbeknown to me, had most likely been heat affected in the back of my vehicle. While the drugs were kept in an esky, the ambient temperature during the day while I was driving would have been forty-four degrees outside. There's every chance it was hotter in the back of my ute under the fibreglass canopy.

My heart aches for the pain that little pony experienced that day. It is never a vet's intention to cause pain or suffering, but as a result of a series of circumstances, my patient suffered that day. It would be nearly twenty years later that I had an experience that made me relate to that little pony.

Alcohol has always been a part of my life. There was never a shortage of alcohol in our house, and I had started to drink to numb the pain of life for the first time as a teenager. From that point on I drank alcohol in different circumstances to calm my nerves, to soothe my social anxiety, to lose enough inhibitions to take to the dance floor; to have fun and to numb the pain. I drank to dull down the emotions that wouldn't leave me alone at night.

My Dad died of alcohol-related illness when Liam was only two. No-one in our family had registered that Dad was an alcoholic until it was written into his medical record when his liver failed. We had lived with it, but had been blind to his addiction.

One day, not long after I had made my commitment to follow Jesus, I was sitting down with my son, Liam, with a photo album across my lap. I was trying to tell him what his grandfather was like. Liam very innocently asked me, 'If you know drinking alcohol is so bad for you, Mum, why do you do it?'

I looked into his searching eyes. I didn't want to tell him the real answer. Perhaps I didn't even recognise that I drank to dull the pain of life. Did I have any idea that I was so scared of the depth of negative emotions lurking in my soul that I spent the best part of my life dulling it down, anaesthetising my hurt? Perhaps not. And for reasons I am still not fully aware of, I made Liam a promise:

'How about I never drink again?'

He looked into my eyes, and smiled and said, 'sure, sounds good', and went off to play with his soccer ball.

I closed the photo album, put it away and I haven't had a drink of alcohol since.

I don't quite know how I managed to give up alcohol after it had been such a large part of my life. I do know that it was a miracle. Jesus stepped into my promise and provided me with the grace to follow through.

What I didn't anticipate was the pain that started to roar through my soul. It was like that pony in stage two anaesthesia on the Members Lawn at Meekatharra. Without the dulling, anaesthetic of an evening wine, the tensions of the day clung to me into the night. I would mull over decisions and conversations and feel the pain of hurtful comments. I would feel the panic of not knowing what was happening, and the desperate struggle to avoid the pain. All of the pain of the childhood abuse, the trauma, the domestic violence and the toxic narrative swirling in my mind came rushing into my consciousness and spilled over into my family life. Like that little pony on the members lawn in Meekatharra, my soul was like a wounded, traumatised and panicked horse, lashing out at people, desperate to run and hide, full of fear.

CHAPTER 24

IN THE ROUND YARD WITH JESUS

*T*he horse stands in the round yard, her head held low. She is standing under the shade of an old flame tree, her skin twitching at flies. Her heart rate increases the moment she sees them. There is a tall stockman, with ropes in his hand. There is another man and a woman. The woman looks somewhat dejected and lost. The horse belongs to her. She has been bucked off so many times she doesn't want to even try again. The pain and anxiety on her face matches the scars that criss-cross the horse. They have both been in a battle. And yet, they are both still alive.

The couple wait outside as the stockman quietly unlatches the gate and steps inside the round yard. The man is entering into the horse's space, and she doesn't like it. Her cortisol rises, the fear and the panic return. She looks for a way out, a way to escape, a way to avoid the man's gaze. His eyes are on her and she trembles. There is *no hostility in his body, his language is love. And still her heart rate pounds out of control.*

Don't touch me.

The stockman approaches the centre of the round yard and flaps the rope against his leg. Instantly the horse whinnies in fear and rears up, before entering a wide-eyed trot as she runs circles around the stockman. She keeps one eye on the stockman, and one eye looking for an escape. He runs her until her heart rate settles into a regular rhythm. He shifts focus and runs her in the other direction. This spooks her and her heart rate skyrockets again for a moment, before settling again. The pattern repeats. The afternoon sun starts to sink towards the horizon as the dust from the round yard hangs thick in the humid air.

The stockman watches the horse's attitude. Her head is low; she is complying with his requests. She is not sure, but she is starting to get curious. What does this man want with me? He stops moving.

It's time to stop running.

Time to let down your guard.

It's okay, you can trust me... he whispers to her heart.

She follows his lead and comes to a stop. She faces up and eyes the man carefully. His body is loose; his hat is low. He has time and she takes it. She slowly, cautiously approaches the man, one step at a time. He waits with his head down, stilling his heart as she stills hers. As she approaches, she can smell his sweet fragrance. The fear remains inside her like a coiled cat, but she takes the last step. She is in his space. His gentle hand cradles her head, as she presses into his chest. She wants to feel his heartbeat.

The stockman whispers a phrase to her, 'Do you want to get well?' (John 5:6)

If the horse was my traumatised soul, representing every broken thought, every hurting emotion, every rebellious idea within me, then the stockman was Jesus.

Mal and I found ourselves in a state of relational dysfunction due the trauma that was sitting in my soul and we needed help. Mal couldn't help me, no matter how much he wanted to fix things. My friends at church couldn't help me. Jesus was asking me a question. I had a choice. In order to get well, I had to submit my soul, full of fear, to Jesus.

Just one touch from Jesus can change your life.

We demolish arguments and every pretension that sets itself up against the knowledge of God, and we take every thought captive to make it obedient to Christ. (2 Corinthians 10:5)

Submitting to Jesus' recovery plan took some time. I went to a range of different Bible study groups, and I went to a survivors of childhood trauma group. Whenever I was driving, I listened to Christian podcasts or worship music, and I kept going to church. While I was busy trying to get well, Jesus was standing in the middle of that round yard every day, waiting for me to come to Him, and to follow His lead. He has all the time in the world.

Reading the Bible or listening to a teaching on the Bible was the easiest way for me to identify where I had thoughts that needed be made obedient to Christ. As I listened something would rise up angrily within me, protesting, kicking and lashing out and bucking within me as I took my panic and fear for another lap of the round yard. Verses about the Father's love were the hardest to digest. I had so many thoughts and experiences of my own father's love that were complicated and confusing and so different from the sacrificial love of God. When my soul was bucking and kicking out at fences and trying to escape, the reality on the ground in our house became really hard for the family. Hurting people tend to hurt other people. There were harsh words, shouting matches and unrestrained, unruly emotions that sometimes found landing places on the kids; however, most of the time, they found their way to Mal.

Mal had a unique ability to identify my ungodly thought patterns. He knew the Bible. He had grown up with it. And sometimes when he shared from the Bible, or he shared his opinion, I wanted to turn around and whack him with it. I know he didn't mean to be harsh or insensitive, but that's how I interpreted a lot of his commentary during those years.

The better way was for me to discover these thought patterns for myself and have the argument with Jesus. It was safer for everyone! And Jesus has very broad shoulders. He was not afraid of my volatile emotions, my angry shouting or my desperate questions. He always responded with love.

While I was working in the 'round yard', Jesus was in my ear, offering wise suggestions. One day when I was railing against Jesus on a walk along the beach, He suggested to me that I love Mal the way he needs to be loved. I was incensed. How could you suggest such a thing? Do you know what I have been through? Do you know how hard it is for me to do that? I had a million angry defensive arguments lined up to counter that suggestion. For a long time, I had been contemplating leaving our relationship. It was so painful for me during that time to stay connected, that I actually felt that it would be easier if we separated. That was when I heard Jesus whisper to my soul, 'I will still love you if you leave.'

I stopped where I was on the sand and bent over double. Tears started streaming down my face. Jesus was always going to love me, no matter how pathetic my attempts were to love those around me. In that moment I knew that Jesus' love was unconditional, it wasn't based on my performance or my obedience. I had the promise of His love, no matter what. And that is what gave me the courage to keep trying.

Each thought took some work. There were some big ones in the mix, and they could take weeks or months to take captive. Some of the worst thoughts would escape captivity from time to time and wreak havoc in my soul before I was able to beat them back into submission. Each thought needed to be replaced in my heart by the truth of God's word.

For 'I am not enough' I found...

I can do all things through Christ who strengthens me (Philippians 4:13, NKJV)

For 'I don't feel loved' there's...

For God so loved the world (including me) *that he gave his only son, that whoever believes in him shall not perish but have eternal life* (John 3:16, ESV).

I poured through the Bible, finding counter arguments for every pretension that I had. Then I got busy repeating them over and over in my mind so that eventually the truth would sink into my heart.

And then, sometimes I would be triggered and all bets were off. Sometimes it would be an attitude of a client, sometimes it would be the words of a loved one asking a simple question. Sometimes it would be a boss, enquiring why something hadn't been done before I left for the day.

The horse in the round yard would rear up, her eyes wide and full of fear. The adrenaline and cortisol pumping through her veins gave her the energy she needed to clear the fence. Then she was off, galloping into the wilderness as far as she could, before she dared to look back. She just needed to get away from everyone.

When her lungs were screaming for oxygen and her muscles were exhausted, she would stop, her flanks heaving for air. The stockman would also stop and wait. There was no rush. There was no point trying to chase her at this time. The cortisol had to be processed; the heart rate had to come back down. He needed to be the safe place.

Come near to God and he will come near to you. (James 4:8)

In the wilderness the stockman would wait. It could take hours, days or weeks for the horse to approach again. But he was always there waiting. When the pain from the past and the threat of danger had subsided, the horse would slowly bridge the gap in the wilderness. She would walk gingerly back to the stockman, eyeing him off as she went. A short way off, she would pause and check for tricks, or ropes or any other entanglement… and seeing none, she would step in again. To hear his heartbeat and rest her head on his chest.

Jesus was my safe place, time and time again. Triggers became an opportunity for me to understand that something from the past was still affecting my soul. These triggers were nearly always unexpected and would surprise my family, Mal particularly, because the responses I gave him were always overinflated. He would ask a $10 question and get a $1,000,000 response. The emotions accompanying the trigger were irrational fears. I was not in immediate danger, but my body would recognise a threat and send me into flight mode without consulting me or asking permission.

There was absolutely no point in trying to discuss the triggering issue with me at that point, although Mal, to his detriment, often would. Once the horse bolted, she needed to run. She will only come back to the discussion when there is no sign of the previous threat. While Mal was learning to be a safe place for me, Jesus would often lead me back into the discussion so that we could work on resolving the issue. It sometimes took months, in the beginning. There would be weeks of angry comments, perfunctory conversation and pretending that things were business as usual. As we got better at recognising a trigger point, the time started to reduce to weeks, and then days. Now Mal and I can recognise a trigger as it is building momentum and diffuse the situation, or return to it later. What took months in the beginning can take minutes or hours now. The triggers are still there, but once Jesus has wrangled the thought and the trauma behind it, then it has no power and is diffused. Turns out that as well as a stockman, and a shepherd, Jesus is also a master bomb disposal expert!

CHAPTER 25

GREAT SIGNPOSTS BUT TERRIBLE MASTERS

Traditional methods of training horses to be saddled and ridden is called 'breaking' them in. Thankfully there are now some beautiful, natural horsemanship methods of building a bond with a horse which is so strong that they would trust you in any situation, including being saddled and ridden. My time in the round yard with Jesus was all about trust. Can I believe what He says in the Bible? Can I rely on Him to be my Saviour, my Protector, my Provider, my Healer, my Light and Life? I had to spend time testing, bucking and rebelling against His love and His word, to prove its solidity to myself.

I found Jesus's love to be completely reliable. His word is the truth. Only my willingness to accept it would waver. Taking every thought captive to make it obey Christ is a process. But I believe it's not the end goal for me, or for any of us. Jesus was gently nudging me to get back on the 'horse' of my wild, erratic and volatile emotions and be led by *His* words, not my feelings, not my emotions, not my old behaviour patterns.

The volatile emotional rollercoaster I had been living was sapping my confidence. I didn't really want to deny my emotions either. For years they had kept me safe in a multitude of dangerous situations. Before I mounted my own emotional horse, Jesus had one more thing to show me.

In the stillness of my quiet time with Jesus, the morning was clear and bright, and the sun was just shedding its first light on a dry and dusty landscape. There was enough dew on the ground to give the earth it's special, morning fragrance.

I made my way to the round yard to see what Jesus would be doing today. The black mare wasn't there. There beside the round yard was Jesus. He was saddling the most magnificent white horse I had ever seen. The horse seemed both powerful and calm at the same time, full of vigour and potential. Jesus effortlessly swung a leg over the horse and asked me with a cheeky grin, 'do you want to ride with me today?'

I hung my head. What? On your horse? Jesus... really? Jesus lowered his hand ready for me to grip His wrist as I heaved myself up behind Him. I didn't feel worthy. I didn't feel able. I felt clumsy and awkward. Yet He insisted. I knew the look in His eye meant that there was no escaping. This time it was fear that we were confronting.

I settled in behind Jesus. He was both tall and strong and I felt safe being so close to Him. I wanted to rest my head against Him and just breathe in His goodness. With the most subtle squeeze of His legs, Jesus cued His horse into a walk, and we made our way across the yard and headed for the horizon. Jesus seemed to direct His horse with intention alone. He called over His shoulder 'Are you ready? Hold on!' And before I knew it, we were cantering across the dry Australian outback scrub.

After enjoying the sensation of movement with Jesus on the horse and the wind in my hair, the light seemed to fade, and it was like we were riding into a cloud of darkness. Jesus drew a long, beautifully ornate sword from its sheath on His right side. I hadn't noticed the sword before that moment. My heart was full of terror. What on earth was going on? As we continued on, Jesus pressed the horse into a full gallop, and thousands of snakes started to appear on the ground. They were striking at Jesus's horse and writhing around to position themselves to attack.

Jesus didn't pay attention to the snakes, but the horse did. For every snake that came his way, he positioned a hoof, squarely on its skull. The crunching of the snakes was oddly satisfying, while terrifying at the same time. I gripped on even harder, certain that I didn't want to fall off at this point.

Then, out of the gloom came a terrifyingly huge bull. It had horns that curled up and out of its skull as thick as my legs, and it was nearly the same size as the horse. It lowered its head and pawed at the dirt. I didn't want to watch, but at the same time I couldn't take my eyes off the bull. Seemingly in slow motion, the bull started its charge. Jesus drew His sword and directed His horse at a slight angle to the charge. As we approached, I braced for a horrifying impact. I couldn't see this ending well.

With a deft sidestep, the horse swung around at the pinnacle of the bull's charge and Jesus plunged His sword deep into the bull's chest, splitting ribs and piercing the beast's heart. The bull crashed to an ignominious stop. Jesus swung His horse around and we backed off the bull a few paces. Blood was still dripping off Jesus's sword and the horse was breathing heavily. I slumped against Jesus; the relief was tangible. I had thought the bull would kill us both. I had forgotten for a moment that I was riding with the Son of God!

Jesus turned in the saddle to look me in the eye.

'I myself, will fight for you, you need only to be still' (Exodus 14:14)

The colour returned to the scene, and we walked beside a clear stream. Jesus dismounted and wiped His sword clean. He offered it to me, holding out the sword, balanced on both of His hands.

'It's time you learnt to use this', He said to me, His face full of concern. I tentatively took the sword. It was heavy. So heavy I didn't think I could even raise it in anger.

'Take the sword of the spirit, which is the word of God'. (Ephesians 6:17),

'So that when the day of evil comes, you may be able to stand your ground.' (Ephesians 6:13)

The weight of the sword was profound. Jesus pulled aside a curtain that exposed an alternate reality. It was a city, with grey, dirty streets. There were people in desperate states of illness and poverty. It was like a scene from a war movie after the devastation of the conflict. People needed to rebuild. People needed to feel loved. People were hurting. 'Take the sword, and go,' Jesus encouraged me, as I paused at the threshold.

It's one thing to be mounted on a white horse behind Jesus, it's another thing entirely to heft the sword of the word of God and walk back into day-to-day life. Knowing that He would fight for me was reassuring. How many more bulls were out there though? Would I need to crush the heads of the serpents too? I didn't feel capable, worthy or qualified to carry His sword, but yet He insisted.

The next morning, we were back in the round yard. The black mare was saddled and waiting patiently beside Jesus. She lifted her head as I approached. Jesus smiled as I walked towards the yard. 'You're ready,' he said encouragingly as I greeted the horse and ti-

died the messy lock of mane between her eyes. Nothing about me felt ready, but I knew I could trust Jesus.

I led the mare into the round yard, Jesus taking His customary spot in the middle. He steadied the mare and held her head as I mounted and took my place in the saddle. My emotions, my thoughts, my attitudes and my desires were under my control. I felt a little uneasy in the saddle and took the reins, remembering what they felt like in my hands. It had been a while. Looking away from Jesus, I squeezed the mare into a trot and started to make my way around the round yard. I found my rhythm, rising and falling as the mare picked her way through the sand. It wasn't seamless, but I was doing it. Take every thought captive to obey Christ. If you have a bad thought, replace it. Remember the words, remember the sword.

The mare baulked as a flower fell off a flame tree, but I responded to her sidestep and squeezed her again, to continue on. There was no deviating, no baulking, no rearing, bucking or escaping on the cards. The peace of the Holy Spirit in me was on this horse, and I settled my heart rate. We can do this; I told myself over and over again.

The concept of choosing your own thoughts was a novel one for me. I had always had thoughts and had never considered where they came from. I was fully aware that some thoughts were helpful, and many thoughts were unhelpful. Thoughts of failure, fear and the great 'what if' never helped me to feel good. If I had those thoughts, I could bring myself back to the place in the saddle behind Jesus, knowing that He would fight for me. I could remember His love, that withstood every angry kick and buck. I remembered the sword which is the word of God.

I can do all things through Christ who strengthens me. (Philippians 4:13, NKJV)

I am fearfully and wonderfully made. (Psalm 139:14)

I am above and not beneath; I am the head and not the tail. (Deuteronomy 28:13)

If God is for me, who can be against me? (Romans 8:31)

I am more than a conqueror and gain a surpassing victory through Christ who loves me. (Romans 8:37, AMPC)

God has chosen me. He has called me by name, he has redeemed me, he has pulled me out of the pit. (Isaiah 43:1)

God's love has been poured out in my heart through the Holy Spirit. (Romans 5:5)

God holds me in his right hand. (Psalm 63:8)

No weapon formed against me will prosper. (Isaiah 54:17)

My inheritance is peace, righteousness, security, victory, love, acceptance, joy and strength. (Romans 14:17)

Jesus is enough. (2 Corinthians 12:9)

God has given me everything I need. (2 Peter 1:3)

Little by little, I was being transformed by the renewing of my mind. Replacing one thought at a time, killing the snakes and mighty bulls that would rush at me in the darkness. I was cleaning off the mud and lifting my chin to face a new day. Jesus opened the gate to the round yard, and I stepped out of the safety of the confined space into a beautiful new possibility, where Mal and Liam and Olivia were waiting with big beaming smiles. The greatest gift I could ever give my family is a gift of wholeness, a gift of self-control and restraint of my own emotions. The very best version of myself is still the greatest gift I can give my family. And today will always be a better version than yesterday if I continue to work with Jesus in the round yard.

GOD'S WAY IS BETTER THAN MY WAY

I would like to be able to say that the transformation of my mind took a neat, linear trajectory to wholeness and wellness; but life is seldom neat, in my experience. Mud is more familiar to me than order and neatness. And while I started to experience the peace that surpasses all understanding (Philippians 4:7), I wasn't able to hold onto it for long. The mental pathways of pain and trauma were neurological superhighways in my life. It was not a twelve-step process.

One day while I was in worship at church, I asked God to fill in my pit. I was so sick of falling back into the pit and being consumed by negative thoughts. I was being plagued by fears and covered in the mud of my past experiences, including shame and guilt, whenever I fell or failed in any way. Because God is faithful, and He heard my prayer, He took me to another beautiful quiet place.

This time I was driving in the outback, a wide-open dirt road in front of me, my favourite music playing loudly in the cab of my Hilux. I was alone, comfortable in the isolation of the desert. I pulled off the road onto a side track and found my way to a great cavernous pit. It was like a roadside quarry. Beside the pit was a shovel and a correspondingly mountainous heap of gravel. This was the pit I kept falling into. This was my pit. Before asking God what He wanted me to do, I saw the shovel. I am up to this task I thought, and I will continue to work until I get the job done.

With all of my bristling independence and self-sufficiency, I started shovelling dirt. It was hot, but I was up for the challenge. I started shifting dirt from the mountain into the pit. The pit was deep. There was a delay as the rocks fell to the bottom of the pit. Hours into the task I was starting to lose hope, but I was determined never to fall into my pit again. Looking for alternate solutions, I cast my eyes around the landscape. Parked behind my mountain of dirt was a D8 grader. I climbed up into the cab without a second thought, turned the key and started pushing the mountain of dirt into the pit.

I was feeling pretty proud, as I completed the task in the comfort of the air-conditioned cab of the grader. That's right I thought to myself, work smarter not harder. It took me no time at all to completely fill in the pit. I stepped down from the cab and looked at the newly worked earth with a glowing sense of satisfaction. My pit was gone. All that remained were a bunch of tracks, criss-crossing the compacted earth, where the pit used to be.

I didn't stand in my glowing sense of satisfaction for long. Jesus came and stood beside me, and folded His arms, surveying my handiwork. He looked at me and His words struck deep into my soul.

'Why didn't you ask me what I wanted to do?'

I realised in that second that I was still operating in my own strength. I had asked God to fill in my pit. And I hadn't paused long enough to give Him an opportunity to do it. I wished in that second that I could erase all of my self-effort, my striving and self-sufficiency.

I hung my head, once again disappointed with myself.

Jesus eyed me quizzically. 'I wouldn't have done it that way'. It was a phrase that was frequently heard in my family of origin, mostly when someone was in some kind of difficulty, usually of their own making, particularly if they had bogged a vehicle or had foolishly run out of fuel.

'This is what I would have done'... The cavernous pit was instantly empty again. All of the dirt, the shovel and the D8 grader were gone. I stared once more into the cavernous pit, full of lurking spiders and snakes and thick, sticky mud right down at the bottom. I was staring at my fears, my guilt, my pain, my disappointments, my disillusionment, my frustration, my disgust, all wrapped up in one smelly, mirey pit.

And then beautiful clear water started to bubble up from the depths of the pit. The mud was swept up and evacuated, along with every foul thought, venomous snake or dangerous spider. The water kept on coming and the pit was flushed clean, until the water was as clear as any water I have ever looked into. I could see the beautiful contours of the pit through a completely different lens. The water was deep enough to have a glorious blue green tinge to it, with shafts of light playing in the depths. And there was still water pouring into the pit. The pit was full to the brim and then it started to overflow. First, a trickle of water formed a little rivulet, meandering across the baking earth into the desert, until it wore a steady path into the interior. The earth soaked up the water.

Just as in a time-elapse movie, I saw grasses and wildflowers start to line the banks of the river. There was a buzz of life, flowing from my pit to make the desert a place of green, luxurious life. It was truly beautiful. There is nothing quite as startling as an oasis in the desert. It is both surprising and precious, a source of life for many creatures. Everyone in a dry place needs water.

Jesus wanted to use my pit to nourish others. He wanted to take the things that I would prefer to hide, to share with others... people that needed a drink, because they were in a dry place. I humbly realised that it was both stunningly beautiful and it wasn't about me. I instantly recognised the truth in that devotional that I had nearly thrown out the window all those months ago. It was not about me...

Listen to me, you who pursue righteousness and who seek the Lord: look to the rock from which you were cut, and to the quarry from which you were hewn; look to Abraham your father and to Sarah who gave you birth. When I called him he was only one man, and I blessed him and made him many. The Lord will surely comfort Zion and will look with compassion on all her ruins; he will make her deserts like Eden, her wasteland like the garden of the Lord. Joy and gladness will be found in her, thanksgiving and the sound of singing. (Isaiah 51:1-3)

Whoever believes in me, as scripture has said, rivers of living water will flow from within them. (John 7:38)

It is my hope that by sharing my story, I might bring light to dark places in other people's lives. One of the deepest pits that any of us face is a feeling of isolation, that we are alone in our pain. Pain isn't a great topic of conversation in the workplace, and it can certainly wear thin with friends too. Living and working alongside people who are hurting is extremely challenging. But there is absolutely a pathway out of pain. I want to be clear that there is no specific formula to follow. Your path will be different from my path. But the narrow path does bring peace and joy and light back into your life, no matter what you have been through.

CHAPTER 27

LIGHT ACCELERATES HEALING

The Hebrew language is a beautiful language, rich in meaning though oftentimes poor in words. When there are fewer words in a language, each word will often carry multiple meanings. Translating the Bible is a difficult task for people with years of study in theology and languages and is often done by large teams. Currently there are many translations of the Bible, and each translation has its own feel, and the same passages of scripture can be translated slightly differently to convey a different emphasis, depending on the meaning implied in the Hebrew word in Scripture being translated. Understanding the Hebrew language for myself has unlocked some really important keys to my study of the Bible.

By far, my favourite word is *shalom*. It is most often translated as 'peace'. However, there is so much more meaning in the Hebrew word *shalom*. First of all, it means 'hello' and 'goodbye'. As well as a greeting, it conveys a deep sense of wellbeing and wellness - nothing missing, nothing broken. The meaning of *shalom* stretches far beyond the mere absence of war, to encompass restoration, reconciliation and rehabilitation.

I have been a student of rehabilitation for over a decade. At the same time, as I took a deep breath and plunged down the waterslide of faith, I also changed the focus of my career to veterinary rehabilitation. I have been learning about the restoration of normal function in both a veterinary sense and in the sense of my own body, soul and spirit. The same principles that apply to the natural world, and certainly the animal world, apply to repairing the wounds of a lifetime of trauma and abuse of the soul.

I have a very comforting chart in my veterinary rehabilitation rooms that is a graphic display of the healing times of skin, muscle, tendon, bones and ligaments. It helps to set an expectation of recovery and the amount of time and effort that may be involved to return to normal function. These can vary depending on whether I am dealing with an exuberant and joyful golden retriever with joint pain or a wise old poodle who has a broken leg, but the guidelines hold fairly true.

The rehabilitation of a soul is a different matter entirely, even though the principles of healing are very similar. The time frames are on a completely different scale. If I was a mathematician, I might be able to tell you what that formula is. What I do know is that it is a much slower process than we anticipate, and there is possibly no formula.

The pain of recovery for physical injuries and soul injuries is real. I did discover at some point in the last few years that paracetamol can treat the pain of wounded emotions and soothe the pain after a traumatic triggering event, in the same way it treats the pain of a headache. The process of recovery itself can be painful, but while I was doing the work and I entered into the process - every time I stepped into the 'round yard' with Jesus—I walked out a little more whole, carrying greater confidence and renewed hope for the days ahead.

While I was working towards the rehabilitation of my soul, my veterinary patients were teaching me a lot about life and recovery. Dogs are truly beautiful creatures. They have a spark of joy and an exuberance for life that we can all borrow from. We really don't know how dogs perceive pain, but we know that they do. The interesting thing about dogs is that they don't seem to be burdened by the psychological element of disease. They don't seem to dwell on the fact that they have a sore knee or that they can't use their legs properly. They just try to figure out how to do those things again. They nearly always work beautifully well with food encouragement and consider the whole rehabilitation process a great game, involving goodly quantities of delicious BBQ chicken.

I believe dogs have a few core beliefs. Firstly, most dogs believe that they are gifted natural athletes. Getting them to stop and rest is the greatest challenge facing most owners with a pet in recovery, especially after major orthopaedic or spinal surgeries. The second is that being with their human is their one main goal. And somewhere in between those two, food plays a big role... especially for labradors. They worship food like no other breed!

Veterinary rehabilitation is a beautifully fulfilling process involving enticing veterinary patients in recovery to exercise and restore function after surgery, using food-based rewards, and then teaching their owners to do the same at home. I incorporate massage as a beautiful way to work through triggers and sore spots because the injury is only part of the way that the body is compensating and adapting to pain. Massaging out the sore spots of compensatory muscle pain is always key to recovery.

One of the other ways we can bring healing in veterinary medicine is with laser therapy. While I was just starting out in veterinary rehabilitation, I had a patient that taught me a lot about never giving up.

Locka was a beautiful border collie with a wise head on his shoulders when he came into the hospital. He had suffered a gruesome injury. He had been run over by a car, in slow motion, in the driveway. His front leg had been trapped under the wheel. While he didn't have any broken bones, the weight of the car over an extended period of time had crushed the tissues. Large areas of skin and muscle were dying. There was also nerve damage to the leg and Locka couldn't put any weight through his paw. The combination of these injuries meant that Locka's whole body was in a fight for his life in intensive care for the first part of the week after his admission, due to the toxic breakdown products in his bloodstream.

His owners were desperate to save him and to save his leg. The surgeon in the hospital was counselling the owners towards amputation when they came to see me. We started an intensive course of laser therapy and worked with the leg to keep the joints moving. We also began to massage and mobilise oedema fluid, trying to restore some circulation and remove the excess swelling.

In between laser therapy sessions, Locka was bandaged with Manuka honey over the large areas of open skin. I was concerned that he may need a skin graft, because the wounds were so large. But under the light of the laser treatment, Locka began to heal. The large open wounds started to close up and the dead skin and tissue quickly sloughed off, revealing healthy healing tissue underneath. Through it all, Locka was amazing. He tolerated the treatments and the therapy in hospital for nearly two weeks.

It became clear around that time, that he was missing his owners. Many dogs feel distressed and anxious without their owners, but Locka actually became depressed and wasn't eating. So, he was discharged from hospital and treated as an outpatient, which lifted his spirits considerably. The laser continued and his skin healed. It was like watching a miracle take place before our eyes. The only problem was that the nerve damage was still not resolving. Nerves are slow to heal and often don't heal. We continued to laser the limb, hoping that the laser therapy would support the nerves in recovery.

Disaster struck when we were five weeks into Locka's recovery. Back on his farm, he had been managing well on three legs, until he tripped and ruptured his cruciate ligament. The injured back leg was diagonally opposite his injured front leg. We were all devastated. I didn't know how we could get him through his ACL recovery while his opposite front leg was still not weight bearing. His owners were determined to try, so Locka had his ACL surgery, and we all waited to see what would happen.

The next day, as he was being taken for a toilet walk outside the hospital, Locka started to use his front leg again. At first, he just started to put his foot to the ground and then he started to take a good amount of weight through it. It was only six weeks since his accident and it was day one after his ACL surgery. I had never before seen that sort of recovery. Locka went on to make a full recovery in both legs and continued to live out his days on his owner's farm, enjoying all of the activities he had enjoyed before.

Locka taught me that sometimes the miracles are just beyond what we think is possible; we just have to keep pursuing recovery. At the same time, I asked God 'How is that possible?' And he whispered to me 'Light accelerates healing'.

When Jesus spoke again to the people, he said, 'I am the light of the world. Whoever follows me will never walk in darkness but will have the light of life.' (John 8: 12)

In my own experience, it was the light of Jesus, the light of life itself that had accelerated my healing process. Being in His presence, going to church and letting worship music wash over me, asking questions, reading the Bible and spending time in meditation and listening for what God was saying, was the way I allowed the light into the darkest places of my soul.

Jesus is often referred to as a shepherd in the Bible; indeed, He said, '*my sheep hear my voice, I know them, and they follow me*' (John 10: 27). Hearing God's voice or Jesus' voice has been the focus of my healing journey. I need to know what God says about me in the Bible, and I also need to hear His direction for today.

God knows what you need before you ask for it, and He knows what you need today. He knows what you need to hear, and He understands all of your pain and how it has affected you through your life.

The original sin in the garden of Eden was not Adam and Eve's eating of the fruit that God had told them not to eat. The sin was that Eve listened to the wrong voice. That same voice comes to kill, steal and destroy every good thing we had in the garden of Eden. It's a voice of deception and it brings death.

We all hear voices; some are internal (mine were extremely destructive) and some voices are external. What we listen to has a huge impact on our daily reality.

Charles Swindoll said, 'Life is 10% what happens to you and 90% how you respond to it.'

I caused myself a world of pain, listening to the wrong voices. Sometimes those voices are embedded into our narrative as children, and they are by far the hardest words to dig out. Some of the words we are listening to today are just as toxic, though. Social media has an endless flow of comparison, condemnation, coercion, control, manipulation, fear, criticism, rejection and more, depending on your level of involvement. Sometimes the voices that influence us are passively and unintentionally absorbed into our soul from the environment we live in, or work in or play in.

The question is, does your internal narrative serve you well, or is it harming you? The good news is that you have a choice. What you absorb into your heart and your belief system is your choice. You can choose what you believe.

I have come to understand that the word of God, the Bible, is truth, even though I don't understand everything in it. The things I have tried and tested have been true. God is love and He is faithful. It would take more than one lifetime to test it all, so I sit in the uncomfortable tension of not having all the answers but trusting that God does.

Trauma is experienced differently by everyone. How we respond or think about the things that happen to us in life will either bring us joy or pain. Burying the pain is not an option. It will surface at some point in your life. When it surfaces, it is important to get help to deal with it. Sometimes the people who are closest to us are the ones that we hurt the most. Pain is difficult to bear and it's easy to offload it on other people. It is true that people who are hurting are the ones who are most likely to hurt others.

In order to minimise the damage to your loved ones, family and friends, it is my strong recommendation that you find the support you need. Our pain is our responsibility. Talking about it, whinging, whining and complaining about your situation will not lift you out of the pit. You need to ask for help from the right places.

I believe partnering with Jesus in your pain is the wisest decision you could ever make. And getting help from people who have walked a similar path to you, and are walking now in victory and freedom, can also be extremely helpful. One of the most helpful things I did during my recovery journey was attend a support group for survivors of childhood sexual abuse. Again, knowing that you are not alone is so validating.

CHAPTER 28

FOR VETERINARIANS

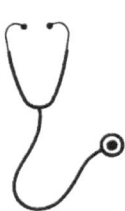

The veterinary industry has a very special place in my heart. It was a very challenging career choice but an extremely rewarding one. I have worked in many clinics and facilities around Australia and the UK with vastly different working conditions and resources and have enjoyed aspects of all of them. I am particularly fond of the people I have worked with along the way.

But there is a common thread amongst the veterinary population that is in desperate need of attention. I gravitated towards working with animals because I wasn't super fond of people. I had been hurt by authority figures in my life whom I should have been able to trust. So, I imagined a life working with dogs or large animals in the bush, having very little to do with people. I didn't know at the time that my pain was driving this career choice. The things I dreamed of when I chose veterinary science turned out to be drastically different from the reality of my veterinary working life.

Being a veterinarian is a demanding, caring profession which requires high level communication skills and empathy. Dealing with people is the main part of the consultative process. Helping animals is the avenue by which you are actually helping people. Helping people day after day without a personal resource to do so is nearly impossible. You simply can't give out of an empty cup.

I carried childhood trauma into my working life and tried to ignore it and hide it for years. It burst to the surface like a festering boil in the midst of my busiest family season, when I was trying to manage young children, searching for that elusive work-life balance. Maintaining a fulfilling relationship with my husband at the same time seemed like a goal that was simply unattainable for me. When you have an 'empty cup' you can't give enough to anyone, not to family, children, partners and clients and work colleagues. When the cup is dry, squeezing it won't help.

The veterinary industry is full of intelligent, capable people, yet the veterinary population is four times more likely to commit suicide than the general population. This breaks my heart. I have lost colleagues to suicide. These beautiful people had so much to give to our world, the loss is unbearable, every time.

While the Australian Veterinary Association is working hard to put programs in place to help vets who are struggling, it is my heart's desire to bring a faith-based solution to the table. I know that Jesus hauled me out of a bottomless pit at a time when some of my colleagues may have chosen to end their life. It's worth talking about.

The statistics for survivors of childhood sexual abuse are not great. Fifty percent of marriages end in divorce in the general population. For survivors of childhood sexual abuse, the rate of divorce is over ninety percent. Similarly, it is statistically very unlikely for rape victims and survivors of domestic violence to manage a marriage relationship successfully. Addiction complicates the numbers significantly.

I would like to say I have navigated addiction, abuse, domestic violence and a career at the same time, but it has not been in my own strength, or my own determination, or my own clever plan that has brought me through it. I have surrendered my life to Jesus. I have invited Him to take the reins of my life. And in doing so, He has crafted a restoration plan for my life that brings me joy, makes me smile and makes me endlessly grateful for the goodness that He has brought to my life. It's not always easy, and I am still processing triggers and pain as Jesus directs me to. I am still married. My kids have lived through it all and they are wonderful, caring, thoughtful human beings. It is a miracle and His name is Jesus. There is untold power in that name. My surrender and His supernatural ability have given me a new perspective and a new purpose to continue living. My strong advice is, if you don't like your life, before you take matters into your own hands... give it to Jesus. He can figure it out for you.

I also want to be very clear that you don't need to suffer through domestic violence or childhood trauma to be traumatised. Trauma can be uniquely personal. Sometimes, the events that traumatise one individual do not affect another. In the veterinary industry, there is plenty going on, from day to day, that can be traumatic events. Stage two anaesthesia in an equine patient was particularly traumatic for me. Working in isolation in the outback was traumatic, particularly when I was doing a surgery for the first time, with no-one there to help or support me. Again, it's not specifically what happens that can be traumatising, it's how we respond to it that can determine how we walk forward from that event.

INNER HEALING

I believe that some injuries require a spiritual solution, not a physical solution. Wounds to the soul fall into this category.

Medicine, as much as I love it, doesn't have all the answers for every injury.

True healing for injuries to the soul comes from being transformed by the renewing of the mind.

As much as I believe in medicine, Jesus is my healer.

Developing a working relationship with Jesus is at the core of my recovery and restoration. I am still learning, growing and understanding God's plan and purpose for my life, including wholeness and wellness, nothing missing, nothing broken, nothing less than the complete restoration of my soul.

The truth of this beautiful reality is that God wants the best for you too. If you have experienced trauma, sexual abuse, domestic or other violence, if you have been hurt in any way and are looking for answers, I can tell you that God loves you and what He has done for me, He will do for anyone who asks.

The testimony of Jesus is the spirit of prophecy. What Jesus has done for me, is available to you. All you have to do is ask.

Getting started is simple. Invite Jesus into your life.

Jesus is God's son. He came to take away the sin of the world. That means that the consequences of sin landed on His shoulders and the price for sin has been paid by Him. The sins we commit, the sins committed against us and the sins committed around us are all covered by the blood of Jesus. God gave us Jesus to solve the problem of sin in the world. Our job is to believe in Jesus and receive the gift.

Jesus also took away illness and suffering - by His stripes we *have* been healed.

It's time to appropriate a better life. Ask Jesus to come into your heart and your life, and I know you will be blessed. The journey is never easy - but doing it with Jesus makes it possible.

Be transformed by the renewing of your mind and you will see God's good and perfect will for your life. God is good… and the gift of life is precious. God has a plan and a purpose for your life.

You are loved and accepted, just the way you are. You don't have to have everything in order to start your relationship with God. There is nothing that you have experienced that Jesus doesn't understand. He took *all* suffering on the cross, so that you could walk in freedom.

He wants you to be free indeed.

We live in a hurting world. Around 1 in 5 girls and 1 in 20 boys are victims of childhood sexual abuse. It's hard to love others when you hate yourself or are consumed by shame.

Nearly 1 in 4 women experience domestic violence. Around 50% of all marriages end in divorce.

Alcohol and drugs may numb the pain for a moment but can become the source of pain in the long run.

Are you looking for another way? Jesus can show you another way, if you ask Him. And He will, because He loves you, He forgives you, He sees how special and unique and valuable you are, and He aches when you are hurting.

APPENDIX

Getting Help - Resources

If you want to know Jesus, can I suggest that you read the Bible? It sounds obvious, but it's true that God speaks to us through His Word. If reading the Bible on your mobile device is more convenient than opening a printed version, there is a free online app that is a great starting point. It's called *YouVersion*, and you can download it from your app store. Within the app there are multiple translations of the Bible, along with daily encouragement and Bible studies.

Another wonderful resource for those that don't love reading but want to watch a movie or dramatized series that presents the Jesus story, I can highly recommend:
The Chosen - watch.thechosen.tv
It is a crowd-funded drama of the life of Jesus, and it's available to download for free on The Chosen app.

If you would like to know more about Jesus from an evidence-based point of view, there are some great books available:
Evidence that demands a verdict: Life-changing truth for a sceptical world, by Josh McDowell.

The Reason for God, by Timothy Keller (and numerous other titles by the same author)

The Case for Christ, by Lee Strobel (and numerous other titles by the same author)

This book also had a major impact on my journey:

The Purpose Driven Life, by Rick Warren.

Another wonderful resource is the Koorong bookstore. You can find your nearest Koorong store location. and access the store online at koorong.com.

For people recovering from childhood abuse, I have found the ministry of Joyce Meyer to be life changing. She has written dozens of books and has podcasts and Bible studies. She has walked the journey of sexual abuse and has a great number of extremely helpful resources for survivors. One of the best places to start is with her book, *The Battlefield of the Mind*, and her webpage - JoyceMeyer.org.

If you have made the decision to follow Jesus, find yourself a local church. We are wounded in isolation, and we heal in community. The Christian journey is meant to be walked out in community. Keep looking until you find the right fit for you.

If you have made the decision to follow Jesus and want to hear God's voice for yourself there are a staggering variety of very helpful resources. I would suggest these are places to start your google search:

Roma Waterman: Heartsong Prophetic Alliance (Melbourne)

Faylene Sparks: Company of Seers (Brisbane)

Prayer ministry can be a powerful key to finding inner healing or healing for your soul. It is like counselling with another Christian, but it is so much more power than just counselling. It is supernatural counselling. Prayer is the opportunity to seek God for His answers in our personal situation and ask for His help. All sorts of things happen when we ask God to help us.

There may be different options available in your area: -

VMTC Ministries: vmtc.org.au (Australia Wide)

Ellel Ministries Australia: ellel.org (Menangle, NSW)

If you ask at your local church, there will be people able to point you in the right direction.

I pray that wherever you are in your journey that you would find peace for your soul, a peace that surpasses all understanding and a peace that gives you glorious rest. I pray that you would know how much you are loved by God, and I pray that you would have an experience of His love that transforms your life. I pray that you would be transformed by the renewing of your mind.

www.ingramcontent.com/pod-product-compliance
Lightning Source LLC
Chambersburg PA
CBHW061207070526
44583CB00025B/3152